# The
# Commitment
# Engine

# The
# Commitment
# Engine

**Making Work Worth It**

**John Jantsch**

Portfolio / Penguin

PORTFOLIO / PENGUIN
Published by the Penguin Group
Penguin Group (USA) Inc., 375 Hudson Street,
New York, New York 10014, U.S.A.
Penguin Group (Canada), 90 Eglinton Avenue East, Suite 700,
Toronto, Ontario, Canada M4P 2Y3
(a division of Pearson Penguin Canada Inc.)
Penguin Books Ltd, 80 Strand, London WC2R 0RL, England
Penguin Ireland, 25 St. Stephen's Green, Dublin 2, Ireland
(a division of Penguin Books Ltd)
Penguin Books Australia Ltd, 250 Camberwell Road, Camberwell,
Victoria 3124, Australia
(a division of Pearson Australia Group Pty Ltd)
Penguin Books India Pvt Ltd, 11 Community Centre, Panchsheel Park,
New Delhi–110 017, India
Penguin Group (NZ), 67 Apollo Drive, Rosedale, Auckland 0632,
New Zealand (a division of Pearson New Zealand Ltd)
Penguin Books (South Africa) (Pty) Ltd, 24 Sturdee Avenue,
Rosebank, Johannesburg 2196, South Africa

Penguin Books Ltd, Registered Offices:
80 Strand, London WC2R 0RL, England

First published in 2012 by Portfolio / Penguin,
a member of Penguin Group (USA) Inc.

10  9  8  7  6  5  4  3  2  1

Library of Congress Cataloging-in-Publication Data

Jantsch, John.
    The commitment engine : making work worth it / John Jantsch.
        p. cm.
    Includes index.
    ISBN 978-1-59184-487-7
    1. Customer loyalty.   2. Corporate culture.   3. Organizational behavior.   4. Commitment
(Psychology)   I. Title.
    HF5415.525.J36 2012
    658.8'343—dc23                                                                2012027025

Printed in the United States of America
Set in ITC New Baskerville Std
Designed by Pauline Neuwirth

 To Carol—Completely

# Contents

## Part 3:

## The Promise: Community

# Preface

> A man's work is nothing but this slow trek to rediscover, through the detours of art, those two or three great and simple images in whose presence his heart first opened.
>
> —*Albert Camus*

**Out of the chaos** something remarkable emerges.

I've owned my own business long enough to have experienced many things. I've seen what happens when I'm impatient, when I try to be something I'm not, when I trust my gut, when I overcome fear, when I wait something out, when I start something, when I finish something, when it's time to move on, what it's like to start over, what it's like to commit fully, and what it's like to let go and embrace the unknown.

I've also experienced countless businesses tied to the notion that growth comes from control and order.

Mostly, however, I've come to recognize that if there's no tinge of chaos, no doubt about what's going on around us, and no lingering sense of unknown, nothing magical will happen.

I'm going to propose throughout this book that in order for commitment to take hold you must first embrace letting go. In a way, this book is meant to generate as many questions as it provides answers, and this may require that you throw out preconceived notions about building a business or, at the very least, be open to exploring that nagging feeling that something is holding your business back.

I believe anyone has the ability to create the most remarkable business they can imagine, and to do so only requires letting go of the need for what most define as order. Often we are so afraid of our own chaos that we try to copy the rules, methods, and processes of others in an attempt to mask our fear.

We fear above all else that this chaos might make us look foolish as we attempt to fashion something that we hope actually looks like art.

It is this same fear that leads us to generate businesses that are lifeless and dreary. And then we wonder why there is no staff or customer commitment—why no one cares as much as we do.

I'm not suggesting that we throw all process and organization to the wind, invite turmoil, and intentionally build businesses that don't serve or survive. I am suggesting, however, that the chaos we think we feel is actually a laughing, singing, dancing, and remarkable order of its own.

If we can only find a way to embrace *this,* the businesses we build could be the kind that feed the heart and soul of everyone who comes into contact with them.

This is real-life strategy, this is joyful culture, this is a committed customer, and this is the essence of a business that's truly alive. Embrace it and use it as your guide.

# The
# Commitment
# Engine

# Introduction

**A business is only alive** to the extent that there is commitment.

This can be said of the individual elements of any business—the products, the services, the people, the customers, the culture, the story, and the brand. It is, however, how these elements come together and collectively generate commitment that is the ultimate marker of success.

But what is commitment in the context of a business?

It is an elusive quality, nameless in most businesses, and exhibits itself most prominently in the areas of strategy, culture, and community. There is no one device that activates commitment, no one idea or mission statement, but it is intentional, and you can feel it in the people, ideas, processes, and stories in companies that have it.

In order to bring commitment to life, it's essential first to gain clarity—to define it and understand how to use it to bring order out of chaos, and how to nurture and grow it with every action and interaction.

The most critical aspect of commitment is that it cannot be manufactured quickly. It must be carefully cultivated and cared for, just as a tree can only come from the careful nurturing of a seed.

In this book, I'll go as far as to suggest that the search for this

1

thing I call commitment is the central theme of our lives as well as the one timeless way of creating a business that is fully alive.

Without commitment, there is very little reason to start an endeavor, let alone toil away day after day in an attempt to fashion something substantial from the seeds of an idea.

Passion alone isn't enough.

Let me be perfectly clear before I go any further with this idea. It's not enough for *you* to be committed, although this is certainly a vital element, but to build the kind of business this book addresses, it is perhaps even more important that you are able to generate commitment for your ideas, your values, your story, your products, your services, and your way of doing and being in all of the various groups of people that make up your businesses ecosystem.

In short, you and your business must become a commitment engine.

Some people are committed to a business because they have no choice; they mortgaged their house and have a child in college. While that might get you up and out of bed each morning, it's not enough to create something spectacular.

The businesses that enjoy commitment the most radiate and generate loyalty by awakening a sense of internal purpose first and foremost. These businesses then draw from a collection of definable core characteristics both internally and externally. These same characteristics exist in every business to some extent, but the level of personal intention acts as a potent measure of the degree of commitment one company enjoys over another.

These guiding characteristics come to life in the form of habits and define the business through the actions they take when they execute strategy, express culture, and create customer experiences.

This book explores the characteristics of commitment, both yours and your ability to generate it, in order to demonstrate how to build a business that is totally alive through tools that already exist in every workplace: clear strategy, culture, and community.

# Teaching Your Business to Manage Itself

Have you ever encountered a business where everything felt effortless? The experience was perfect, and the products, people, and brand worked together gracefully. You made an odd request; it was greeted with a smile. You went to try a new feature; it was right where it should be. You walked in, sat down, and felt right at home.

At first, building a business can seem a bit like playing with a giant set of LEGOs scattered all over the room. There are countless pieces that might fit together, or they might not, and success depends on using these fragments to create something cohesive that resembles a normal shape or structure.

But here's the thing: Normal is a trap. Normal is the business you ran from to start something new. Normal is the last three ventures that choked and spurted and collapsed under the weight of management. Normal is a poor version of your ultimate goal.

Businesses that run so smoothly as to seem self-managed aren't normal. In fact, they are terribly counterintuitive, but terribly simple as it turns out. The key is to focus all your energy on only three things: clarity, culture, and community.

### CLARITY

Until you are perfectly clear about the one thing your business does better than anyone else, and perhaps more important, the high payoff behaviors that you, as the owner of the business, must spend as much time as possible immersed in, you will have a very difficult time creating something that is graceful and effortless.

Until you can feel why you do what you do best and use that as your guide, the road ahead will always be uncharted.

When you have clarity, everything becomes simple. The solutions to difficult decisions will suddenly seem obvious because you have created the perfect filter and the filter runs the business.

## CULTURE

Every business, regardless of its size, has a culture. The only question is whether or not the established culture serves the business and the people who come to work there. If a business is to manage itself, then a culture of ownership should be the sole objective. This must come at the expense of hierarchy and the assertion of autonomy.

I've worked with business owners for years now, and in my experience, control, or the inability to hand over control, is the greatest threat to growth. Until a business owner can extend trust to those around him and give up control, there will be little more than constriction and contraction.

This means that you must also be able to communicate your sense of clarity and purpose, and present a set of core values that become the road map for culture and the mantra for "this is who we are."

## COMMUNITY

There was a time when the term *community* referred to only the customer. Today the community includes customers, employees, mentors, vendors, advisers, and even competitors conspiring to advance and influence the business ecosystem.

When you have a clear picture of what the business stands for and the people who fill in that picture are given the freedom to manage their results, the natural outcome is a strong, vibrant, and supportive community.

A fully alive, self-managed business is little more than the sum of these parts brought together through a clear purpose.

This book is divided into three distinct parts: the Path, the Patron, and the Promise.

In the **Path,** we'll explore your own sense of clarity and passion, the higher purpose of the business, and the strategies you'll employ to bring purpose alive in your work. You'll also explore the characteristics of what I call real-life marketing strategy. This is the foundation of a committed business.

In the **Patron,** you'll see how these characteristics are shaped into a culture in the hands of a supportive leader and how commitment is then fueled internally. At this point it may actually become unclear whether strategy creates culture or if, in fact, it's the other way around.

In the final section, the **Promise**, we'll explore the idea of creating an environment where your customers experience the characteristics of commitment in an effort to generate the kind of everyday commitment that's necessary to foster extreme customer loyalty, community, and word of mouth.

## Part 1

# The Path:
# Clarity

# 1

# Clarity Over All

**Jason Fried, cofounder of the** software developer 37signals, knows a thing or two about commitment. As any software developer can tell you, it takes real perseverance to make a product that does exactly what someone needs, nothing more and nothing less.

There's always more you can add and more you can make the program do, simply because you have the capability. For Fried, the commitment to clarity is the most important issue in his business. In fact, Fried and the folks at 37signals fret over clarity in a way that has turned it into perhaps their single most important reason for being in business.

"A lot of people talk about our products being simple, and what they really are is terribly clear. We obsess over making everything obvious, even though what it does may in fact be rather complicated," Fried explains.

But first a little background.

In 1999, Fried, Carlos Segura, and Ernest Kim started a Web design firm called 37signals in Chicago out of a desire to, in the words of Fried, "build cool stuff with other people."

In 2003, the company brought in David Heinemeier Hansson to develop a project management tool for managing design projects.

After trying out their homemade tool on behalf of their clients, it became clear that their real mission was to build and deploy a world-class project management system. That next year Basecamp was launched.

Now with over 3 million users and a suite of software applications, this highly profitable company has clearly become a success story.

But what is the secret behind the success of 37signals?

According to Fried, his thirty-person company is consumed by the desire to build tools that people can't imagine working without. This is their purpose and it's created an immense sense of clarity and drive for everyone involved.

## Clarity of Purpose

There are so many important ideas and concepts in business. Things like strategy, purpose, and passion are integral to success, but none of it really matters without one ingredient: clarity.

Clarity is that strong and unwavering sense that our daily choices are grounded in an authentic purpose. Clarity is how we create a sketch of something worth asking others to complete. Clarity forces us to ask the right questions.

Without clarity, everything we do is either an attempt to gain it or a stab at moving in the right direction.

Almost every business I've ever worked with, including my own, has struggled with this idea. Until we have total clarity and are inspired by why we do what we do, whom we do it for, and how to do it with complete and utter honesty, little else matters.

Clarity does not emerge by simply switching on a clear and guiding light. No, it comes when we find a rusty but sturdy lamp in the basement of an old house. A little more comes through when we take the time to bring the lamp into the light of day and clean it up. Then, only through careful tinkering and polishing, this lamp begins to cast a flicker of light.

As we continue to restore our find, something truly brilliant begins to evolve.

With clarity, comes control. With clarity, comes grace. With clarity, comes joy.

Finding and maintaining clarity takes work. It takes an unbending willingness to see things for what they really are. To base decisions on what might be best for others. To understand how to create the products and services our customers really need.

Clarity is both a feeling and a direction. It can be experienced and seen. It is at the same time perfect simplicity and obvious complexity. Clarity inspires us and those around us.

But what is it exactly?

For the answer, I'll return to 37signals.

"People often try to make things that are simple, but sometimes you need things that do complex tasks—the trick is to make the complex clear," says 37signals cofounder Fried.

It's an obsession over every element in the product. Is it clear what this button does? Is it obvious what this tab is for? Does the user know what to do next?

The idea of clarity then runs through every element of the business; it's embedded in the way they talk about their products, market their products, hire new associates, arrange the desks in the office, and even how they price their offerings.

"We want to be very clear about every aspect of our business and it's something that we have to do as leaders by example," explains Fried.

## Clear Intentions Define Commitment

Most businesses are started with the acquisition of a customer in mind and eventually, often through toil and trouble, get around to figuring out how to serve the needs of the owner. I get that; there is no business without a customer.

One of the goals of tackling a wide-ranging topic like commitment is to flip the traditional "get customers first" business model on its head by suggesting that first and foremost a business must be started and grown with the goal of serving the owner's original intention and passion for that particular business.

If a business created in this fashion can then link that intention to a single-minded business purpose, even a purpose seemingly unrelated to the actual product or service, and then use purpose to make a business where people can become fully alive, the only logical end is a loyal, committed customer.

What I suggest is that there is one true committed way to build a fully alive business. There are, in fact, countless ways to build a business, but my contention is that there are common elements, practices, and patterns visible in the fully alive, commitment-filled business that I will discuss throughout this book.

## Meet the "Four P's" of a Fully Alive Business

In order to have total and complete clarity in your business, you also need to be clear on how marketing fits into your overall plan. After all, marketing in its fully realized sense pervades every element of a business in the same way that commitment does. Before we move on, I'd like to introduce a commonly accepted marketing concept to explain one of the elements that is central to the idea of commitment in business.

Using the broadest definition of the term, anything that has even the slightest impact on a customer or prospect is considered marketing. Having a clear understanding of how to combine the notion of commitment with marketing is essential to your success.

Back in the early 1960s, a University of Michigan professor named E. Jerome McCarthy coined the term the *Four P's* as a way to describe the essential elements of the marketing mix. Since then, all first-year marketing students have been taught to think in terms of product, price, place, and promotion as they analyze case studies of companies real and imagined.

Much has changed in the last fifty years, including what a product really is, what place entails, how package plays a role, and pretty much everything about what promotion looks like.

In fact, the very definition of marketing has changed dramatically enough to render the original Four P's somewhat useless as a foundational marketing and business strategy concept.

Today's most important business and marketing directive is to build trust. Creating engagement, connections, and stories are the new forms of promotional art. Price is a function of value and place has become bytes and ether more often than a shelf in a store.

There is a home for the Four P's in today's business, but it's in the very mortar of the business and the story of its people rather than in a department on an organizational chart.

The Four P's are now more about how a business is experienced than what it sells. They reside in the characteristics that turn commitment into culture and culture into a customer.

The following elements redefine the Four P's for the fully alive business, and further make the case that every business is really a marketing business.

## Passion

The first element in a fully alive business is the passion for living that the owner of the business brings to the workplace. Good things happen when the founder of a business can serve his own personal passion and purpose by growing the business.

Your business can be the tool that allows you to live your passion or it can be the vehicle that produces the time, connections, and money that allow you to embrace the "other thing" you know you're meant to do.

Kevin Rains, the owner of Center City Collision, an auto body shop in Cincinnati, freely admits that he bought the company solely as a means to grow his family, reinvigorate his community and neighborhood, and invest money in nonprofits locally and beyond.

According to Rains, his business has grown eightfold over the last eight years due in part to his reinvestment in his local community that includes support for the local service league, a community garden, founding a local rugby league, and buying and renovating three abandoned buildings to house businesses and provide low-income housing.

The business has also allowed him to adopt three children from a special-needs orphanage in Colombia.

Rains's passion is for service and the community, and his business is the tool that allows him to live out his purpose.

The leader of a business must have a great sense of passion for his work, but he also must be able to connect that passion with a purpose in order to bring out the desire to commit in others. Leading with passion is how to put yourself out there and do what you were meant to do.

## Purpose

Purpose is how a business defines why it does what it does. It is the reason people are drawn to work in a business, it's the reason they come to life inside the business, and it's the reason customers commit to and become loyal ambassadors of a brand.

Purpose builds trust between a business and its employees and customers because it allows people to see their own values in action in support of something they strongly believe in. A weekly paycheck, an important promotion, or a great deal on a cool product doesn't invoke much in the way of purpose. You have to go beyond the obvious.

Mary and Tony Miller, co-owners of Jancoa, had a people problem. Their successful janitorial service, located in Cincinnati, had more work coming in than they could handle. Their problem, however, wasn't the result of great marketing generating customers; it was because they couldn't find and keep committed employees. The

Millers started each day about thirty full-time employees short and scrambled all day to get the work done as promised.

They found themselves hiring over fifty new people a month and enduring an industry norm of around 400 percent turnover. One weekend they decided to go to a bookstore and find everything they could about hiring and retaining employees.

One nugget they latched on to was a suggestion that they find and fix the hurdles employees and potential employees faced in order to stay on the job. To that end, Tony decided to buy a van and provide employee transportation between jobs.

While the van didn't solve all their problems, after several weeks of driving through the neighborhoods where his employees lived, the Millers realized that while many of their employees lacked transportation, what they really lacked were hopes and dreams. In their view, life and living and lack of opportunity had robbed them of hope.

Jancoa decided that its "people problem" was really a dream problem and they set out to center the company on its people and their dreams. They began to invest in ways to make employee housing more affordable and promoted GED and college tuition programs.

They even created a program called the Dream Manager and started making dreams and dreaming bigger a part of the everyday culture and language of the company.

Mary Miller tells it like this: "When people decide to go after something bigger, magical things happen. We could have never predicted this to be the outcome, but what we discovered firsthand was that we were able to change the quality of life of our people by changing their view of the future.

"People don't dream about entering the cleaning industry, but now they come to work for us and we tell them give us your best three to five years and we'll help you work your way out of a job."

Jancoa's turnover is down by 45 percent and their Dream Manager program has been chronicled and emulated by organizations large and small around the globe. Over the past few years, Jancoa has grown to a company with more than three hundred employees and annual sales exceeding $10 million.

The Millers found their purpose and passion almost by accident, but they knew it when they saw it. Jancoa is now a "build people up" business disguised as a janitorial service.

Joining a purpose-filled business that is on a journey to create joy, change an age-old industry, innovate, or just do a great deal more of the right thing is more like joining a cause, and people will do some remarkable things in support of their cause.

## (Value) Proposition

Organizations that understand the power of purpose also understand that their unique purpose is what they need to promote as their reason for being, their core difference from their competitors, and use it as a positioning tool in the market on a daily basis.

In fact, brands that start with purpose over product can effectively enter almost any market with the same value proposition and compete with entrenched category leaders. It's become cliché to cite Apple as an example, but this computer company routinely blows competitors away in any market they enter. MP3 players and mobile devices are just two categories they entered and dominated even though they were originally a computer company.

The beauty of creating a value proposition in this manner is that it's not about putting something out there that paints your business in a positive light; it's about doing things consistently that allow you to serve your purpose while helping others get what they want, even if it's unrelated to what your business does.

Matt Brown is an insurance producer in west central Ohio who works at his family's agency. His is a business that's often driven by price, but those who excel understand that it's about building relationships by giving value first.

Matt's customers are mostly small-business owners, so he speaks at local clubs about social media and helps these organizations understand the process and philosophy of the medium: it's not about self-promotion, it's about giving freely.

He then offers to send them a tip every week via his e-mail

newsletter. Funny thing is, he doesn't ever really talk about insurance and yet he's developed a following of small businesses that look forward to his helpful hints each week.

He serves his purpose of helping small-business owners grow by positioning himself as the insurance agent who provides value far beyond what a typical agent would consider is their role.

As Brown says, "My purpose is to help you produce more. My Web site is specifically designed to be a lead generator by giving away value in exchange for a person's attention. And I continue to live out my purpose by sending my subscribers value each week.

"When it's time for these small businesses to renew their insurance policies, I'm the agent they call," he says.

## Personality

The final P is how a business uses desirable human characteristics or personality traits as a vehicle to allow everyone who encounters the business to experience and commit to its purpose.

It's one thing to state your purpose on a plaque or marketing brochure, but it's another thing entirely to live by a tangible set of daily habits, language, and processes that offer proof of that purpose.

We are drawn to people and experiences that are simple, inspirational, convenient, innovative, playful, community-oriented, and filled with surprise. These are the personality traits that a fully alive business incorporates into their everyday language.

These traits act as the filter for every decision, and help decide how the business is run internally and how the brand is experienced externally.

# 2

# Work as Craft

 **Owning a business is a** beautiful thing; a thing done quite often, not for riches, but to fulfill a dream or carry out a passion. Work viewed in this fashion embodies the qualities of a craft: skill, passion, knowledge, pride, and ownership.

Yet these qualities are so easily silenced in the rush of business life. We don't even feel the loss coming, making it even more painful as it goes by largely unobserved.

I meet business owners, employers, and employees all over the globe who tell me that their work is sucking the life out of them and they wonder how it's happened, and how to get back on track to a balanced life.

The first step is to get very clear about your relationship with the work that your business does.

In order for your business to become fully alive, you must become fully alive inside it. Perhaps at this point you have developed passion and desire for your work. Or maybe your commitment stems from a lack of choice—you must make this business work. But, as you may have begun to sense, that's simply not enough.

You must also be able to connect what you do in this business with your own personal goals, desires, and needs. You must understand what you're passionate about. You must be able to establish a clear link between what you want out of life and how your business can play a part in making that come about.

The connection may be obvious; there are cases where the primary purpose of a business can directly serve the primary passion of the individual. For example, a cancer survivor might start a business making stylish clothes for other cancer sufferers as a way to serve a life purpose that chose her.

The connection need not be obvious. You can meet personal objectives by simply creating a business that increases your income, connections, and available time to dedicate to serving your chosen calling. Or you can fulfill your own personal desire to spread happiness by creating a business that focuses on doing just that—even if that business is something not traditionally associated with such an emotion—like dentistry or tax preparation.

Either way, a connection must be present. The never-ending search for and evolution of this connection is where the most growth occurs.

Of course, in order for your business to truly serve your life, you must identify and make a strong commitment to what that means and how this business will ultimately aid you.

Perhaps more than anything else, that is what this book is about because that is what owning a business is mostly about.

Make no mistake: the effort and exploration required to identify and master your own personal commitment is not a "day at the cabin" project. You may start to plant the seeds of intention or uncover a hint of the true meaning that's been lurking in your business all along by going into solitude and quieting the noise momentarily, but this process is very much a work in progress.

The point is to get started now.

It is only through mastering your own commitment that you are free to help others do the same through your business and with your business.

Once you understand the bounds of your own commitment, you can begin to explore and install specific elements as the personality traits of your brand.

We return time and again to the seven characteristics of inspiration, simplicity, play, convenience, community, innovation, and surprise throughout this work in an effort to steel your own commitment and unearth patterns and processes to form a business that generates loyalty in both staff and customers.

## Your Playing Small Doesn't Serve Anyone

The single behavior that prevents business owners, or really anyone for that matter, from realizing the incredible potential that lies in their business is playing small.

Small is easy, small doesn't attract attention, small is comfortable, small doesn't offend, small doesn't raise eyebrows, small keeps that little voice in your head quiet, small doesn't hurt as much when you fall, and small keeps you right where you are.

Thinking small robs you and your business of the art of serving your own personal purpose in life and building a business that inspires others to do the same.

Now, don't confuse this with the idea of growing a big business. What I'm talking about is thinking bigger about what you're capable of, about your role as the inspirational leader of your big idea.

Allowing yourself to think and act greater than you are is one of the greatest ways to tap your own individual potential and build a better you.

The problem with thinking small about things like the higher purpose of your business, what's possible in your business, or the audacious brand you know you can achieve is that you won't be inspired to take massive action.

Think about a goal you've set in the past that you didn't achieve. Why didn't you achieve it? My guess is because it was a small goal. It was likely something you had little trouble imagining you could accomplish, but also something that didn't require you to change much, and so nothing happened.

In order to build a business that inspires you, you need to stir up doubt. In fact, it needs to create enough doubt that you have no idea how it will come to pass. You need to connect with a feeling of purpose that excites and inspires while at the same time making you uneasy.

I'm not suggesting that you make up some audacious, pie-in-the-sky dream. I am suggesting, however, that if your goals aren't big enough, they won't come true.

Let me give you a simple illustration. Let's say you have a business and you commit to increase revenue by 10 percent. Now, you may not know how you're going to get all that new business, but perhaps a tweak here or there to your Web site might get it done.

What if, on the other hand, you committed to triple the revenue you generated this year? You may have no idea how you're going to do that, but would it be safe to say you might start rethinking everything about your business?

What if starting today you looked out three years from now and saw something huge? What if you dared not simply to dream but to accept the awesome potential locked up inside you?

Go ahead, I dare you.

## The Characteristics of Personal Commitment

The characteristics of your own personal commitment differ significantly in some ways from the characteristics used to construct a fully alive business: strategy, culture, and customer.

Consider carefully the impact that the following characteristics have on your initial thinking about your own life and understanding your relationship with the work that your business does.

### PURPOSE

Why am I doing this? That's the question, isn't it? Sure, it's become a cliché in business circles to suggest the need for this, but until you've got it, work will rarely be more than a series of activities loosely tied to a set of objectives.

As you will see as you progress through this book, purpose may be the single most powerful business and life tool you can uncover.

Purpose is the closest thing to a human compass that exists. Yet, so often we go out there in the business jungle without one. Purpose creates passion and passion attracts customers.

Years ago, one of my clients was indicted for some shady business practices. Did I suspect something was fishy? Perhaps. But I know that was the day I vowed never again to let myself work with people I didn't respect.

In fact, my higher purpose was crystallized in that moment. I realized after some soul-searching that my business could be a vehicle to help small-business owners get their lives back. That is what drives everything I do and fills my day with an incredible sense of purpose and meaning.

### LOVE

Thankfully, this is a word we can now use in business without being thought of as weak. Ironically, it takes a great deal more strength to do things in business out of love rather than out of profit, and yet to do so may be the most profitable mindset you can embrace.

I really love the people I work with and for. I love the people who are drawn to my brand and community and the only way that happens is if you continuously communicate what you believe is important.

What does it require to make even the simplest business decisions out of love? It's easy to view a question like this in the romantic sense of love and that's not what I'm referring to here at all.

So, let me restate the question posed above in a slightly different way: what would it require to make even the simplest business decisions out of care and mutual respect for those whom they impact?

You can take the idea of doing things out of love as deep into your business as you like; the only thing your business can't tolerate is indifference.

## WONDER

Some may roll their eyes when I say this, but I wake up every day expecting a miracle, and consequently, I'm rarely let down. I am blessed with an insatiable curiosity and it helps me marvel at all the cool things I get to do as a business owner and earthling.

Sometimes in business we can't control everything that happens, but we can control how we react to and view events. If you choose to let what happens around you be your teacher, you'll end up with an incredible education in a very short time.

This isn't a wide-eyed kind of wonder. This is the kind of faith that's developed by experiencing the payoff that comes from nurturing a commitment to purpose.

How do you start paying attention to the role your thoughts play in your future actions? Can you be more attuned to how you think? Can you begin to make wonder and curiosity a key part of the equation?

## COURAGE

There's a long-standing debate in business circles about the differences between an entrepreneur and a small business. The issue centers on the notion that if you're an entrepreneur, you care about high growth, and if you're a small business, you're somehow destined to struggle to make ends meet while working your fingers to the bone.

Don't most entrepreneurs really just start out as small-business owners?

I'm not a fan of this distinction and from this point forward you won't read the term *entrepreneur* in this book too often. It's not that I have anything against that term other than the perception it creates.

The only real difference between one business and another is how the owner views her business. You can see it as a high-growth machine and still work your fingers to the bone with little to show for your efforts or you can create a small lifestyle business that pays you handsomely and affords you the time to take in the world.

So, what's the difference between a fully alive business and one that is lifeless and dreary?

It's not just about high growth. It's about the owner's courage to commit to a pattern of leadership through constant innovation and a unique way of being and doing that fuels *her* unique definition of growth.

I work with an awesome bike trainer and during tough interval workouts he always reminds us that we should be having some serious doubts and questions while in the middle of what we're doing right then or we are cheating ourselves, but we should still have the courage to face our fears and carry through with our goals. The same challenges will come up in your business on a daily basis.

Your commitment must contain certainty about where you are going while allowing for and accepting a great deal of doubt about how you might get there. It takes courage, but once you accept this, you won't stress about where the growth, answers, or money is going to come from quite as much.

### GRACE

Business can feel like one jagged, lurching ride at times. When you replace doubt with purpose, ambition with love, dread with wonder, and fear with courage, something incredibly graceful can emerge.

A commitment-filled business has a rhythm that is both intimate and elegant and people are drawn to it, not by word or even action, but by something much harder to describe—authenticity.

That's the beauty and mystery behind any fully alive person or business. How they appear when you encounter them may not reflect the years of growth, struggle, soul-searching, and failure that came before.

Grace comes from being comfortable with who and where you are. This is true for your business as well.

If any of the elements in this list has made you even the least bit uncomfortable, or even if it's made you smile with recognition, I'd like you to consider the following question: what are you willing to give up in order to create a commitment-filled business?

We'll come back to that question very soon.

## What I Know for Sure About Work

Since I've owned my own business for so many years, I'm often asked what I've learned over time, which for me is another way of asking about my relationship with the work I do.

The first thing I've learned is that one of the coolest things a business can do is teach us. The only mystery is whether or not we'll let it.

These are the things business has taught me over the years:

### 1. Do Work You're Proud to Finish

I've mentioned it already in this book, and it's a favorite of experts everywhere, but you must do work you love. While I won't argue with the virtue in that, I'll take it a step further. I love what I do, but I get paid for what I finish. It's often that last 10 percent that dictates whether or not a project is a success.

It's very easy to get passionate about a venture in the beginning, but the true measure of staying power is in the pride you feel in seeing something through to the end.

Find work that motivates you to the end.

## 2. Connect Purpose as You Evolve

Everyone talks about finding purpose, but no one's doing anything about it. What you're going to find out in this book is that purpose finds you more than the other way around. In the beginning, it's very hard to know why you're doing what you're doing, but ultimately, purpose will evolve or you'll move on to something else.

We are going to explore what really drives you to do what you do. A higher purpose is what makes owning a business worth it.

But it won't serve you to sweat it; you must simply live it. Purpose, discovery, and development are human alchemy at its finest.

## 3. Serve Customers You Respect

In my first book, *Duct Tape Marketing,* I defined marketing as the act of getting someone who has a need to know, like, and trust you, but I believe the flip side is true as well. In the long run, if you can't attract clients whom you come to know, like, and trust—and ultimately respect—then it's hard to perform in ways that feel very authentic.

I'm not saying that every business owner has to enjoy every customer, but on your journey to create a business where people and customers can become more fully alive, few things create more friction than people who don't share your purpose and commitment.

Great customer service develops most fully from a place of mutual respect.

## 4. Give Wins to Everyone

If I am to be brutally honest here, this one is hard for me. I like to receive credit for things well done, but rarely is anything worth doing accomplished without the help of others.

A business where this dynamic is alive and well creates a positive and vibrant culture. Great leaders are adept at creating strategy, implementing plans, and making the entire team a part of the victory.

The greatest experiences I've ever had in business came when I freely acknowledged the critical contributions of others at every level.

## 5. Learn from Challenges

Over the years, I found that when I had a crushing project, I would occasionally fall into a pattern of procrastination. I used to wonder why I did that, but what I came to understand eventually is that sometimes procrastination serves as a tool for processing information.

Challenges teach us if we let them. It's essential to adopt a mindset that searches out the lesson in every setback.

This is something some people do intuitively, but if that's not you, you've got to find or develop your information sensor and employ it to help you get through times when your work is out of balance.

I spoke in the introduction about the need to embrace chaos. What feels like chaos is often just temporary imbalance, so take it as a useful piece of data instead of as a sign of an impending train wreck.

Process the data by stopping and asking why this or that is happening and what it is here to teach you.

## 6. Grow Through Trust

Yes, you must earn trust—it's essential if you are to build a business—but you must also extend trust.

If you can't trust that others can accomplish tasks, do what they promise, and make good decisions, you'll never grow your business beyond what you can wrap your two arms around. And make sure that your trust issues don't stem from your lack of self-trust.

## 7. Hire Your Blind Spots

If you stay in business long enough, you'll find yourself making the same mistakes over and over again.

You've got blind spots, weak points, and important issues that you don't care to address. One of the core truths about commitment is that it's tough to stay committed and on purpose when doing something that you don't enjoy. You'll find reasons to simply not do the work and thereby create even bigger problems.

Even things you enjoy might be considered blind spots because they rob you of the resources needed to lead an organization. It's absolutely essential that you understand both what you love to do and what you're most valuable doing and work at getting better in that space. Stop worrying about the things you can't do well and hire someone else to do them.

As long as you don't delegate strategy and never actually abdicate anything, you can hire for your own shortcomings and get passionate talent in every corner of the business.

## 8. Become an Elevator

The most rewarding thing I get the chance to do every day is make things happen for other people.

Some great people have helped me over the years and I used to think I'd earned it, but now I know it's just a big part of the cosmic scorecard. Raise others up and the universe will take note.

This might be the single most important strategy you can employ in your efforts to generate commitment in others. People want to go on journeys worth taking, and if you elevate them inside that journey, you allow them to connect in ways that look and feel a lot like ownership.

It wasn't until one of my daughters started to work for me that I fully understood this. With her, I had a lifetime of wiring that told me I was her mentor before I was ever her boss and that view allowed me to appreciate the business leader's role as a mentor.

Don't confuse this thinking with soft-minded, pop management fluff. I'm not suggesting you have to be a parentlike mentor to every employee. But your employees will elevate your customers if you elevate them. I'm pretty sure that's going to pay off handsomely in the end.

## 9. Throw Away the Scorecard

Don't tally your wins, losses, credits, or debits—simply learn from each one. Stay focused on what you believe in and put those beliefs into action every single day.

Scorekeeping tends to cloud your vision of where you really stand in the larger picture.

Focus is your energy engine and it has one job: to keep you on purpose.

You've only got so much energy to burn and you can't waste a moment worrying about what others do or say. Just keep doing what energizes you the most.

## 10. Understand That Culture Equals Brand

You, your people, and your story, that's your brand. Your people will go out into the market and treat everyone they come into contact with in the name of your business precisely as you've instructed.

If you don't respect your customers, don't expect any of your employees to. If you don't respect your employees, know that they will transfer that lack of respect directly to your customers.

Part two of this work is about building culture as brand, but the first step is to accept this as essential business building strategy.

Unless you're Apple, Target, or, say, Procter & Gamble, your brand isn't as much about product design, pricing strategies, brand messages, and advertising as it is about the experience people have when they call your office, visit your store, engage a consultant, or receive your product.

A vibrant, fully alive culture is how you convert just satisfactory into simply exceptional.

### 11. Let People Help You

My final lesson is a hard one. I can't stand to ask for help and yet it's not only the right thing to do in many cases but it's the biggest gift you can offer to others.

By asking for help, you acknowledge the value others can bring, and instill a sense of purpose that is every bit as important as the act of giving.

I hope this chapter has changed or reaffirmed your thinking about your own personal relationship with your business. Now it's time to explore in depth the fire that strengthens your commitment—purpose.

# 3

# The Kiln of Commitment

**In this chapter we go** to work on finding your passion, your commitment, and your mission. But let me be honest; this isn't going to be easy. In all likelihood, if you haven't made a firm commitment to the ultimate purpose you want to serve in your life and with your business, it's because it has eluded you.

The age-old question that pushes you to decide what you want to be when you grow up is still a hard one for you to grasp and perhaps even harder to translate in ways that might make sense to someone else.

Let me assure you, it's there and we're going to find it. But before we do, you've got to understand that some of the conclusions you might draw from this exploration could be unsettling. Maybe you'll decide that you're not doing what you are meant to do, that you're not capable of serving a higher purpose in your business as it exists today, or that you're working with all the wrong people and serving the wrong clients.

Finding passion and purpose in the realization that you must make a drastic change is a gift, not the one you'd hope for perhaps, but a gift in the form of a tool to help you.

You may also find that this chapter reaffirms your love for what you're doing and reignites a fire long since extinguished. Perhaps this chapter will reintroduce you to who you really are and why you really started your business in the first place. This is the promise of a fully alive business. Remember, your business will only come to life to the extent that you do.

Give yourself permission, right now, to take this chapter and the exercises contained in it very seriously. Before we start, let me ask you this: what's going to change in your business and your life if you continue to operate in the same manner you always have.

## Who Are You?

I don't know you and I'm not going to make any assumptions about what's going on in your life or why you're reading this book.

But I do know that people who hold a clearly recognized sense of passion and purpose as their internal compass are much happier than those who merely drift along reacting to the events of the day.*

Now, I'm not talking about your job description, long-term goals, or business strategies. I'm talking about connecting with a global view of why you do what you do, how you want the world to experience you as a person, and the difference you hope to make. Discovering your purpose can become a constant guide through which you filter your thoughts and actions.

This might be a good point to tell you that while I've recognized what I'm most passionate about for many years, act upon it every day, and use it to decide even little actions—I get it wrong as often as I get it right.

That may not be a very good way to sell you on this idea, but I also know without hesitation that I would get it wrong 100 percent of the time if I didn't call upon passion and purpose to guide me. I attribute

---

* C. M. Youssef and F. Luthans, "Positive Organizational Behavior in the Workplace: The Impact of Hope, Optimism, and Resilience," *Journal of Management* 33 (2007), 774–800.

any amount of success I've achieved in business to clinging tightly to an idea that excites me.

From a purely pragmatic standpoint, connecting with a powerful passion and purpose can simplify things. When you have to make a tough decision, you turn to your purpose for clarification. Eventually, through time and use, you'll learn to make the right decisions.

## Why We Can't Commit

There are a couple of reasons why people don't use this idea of personal commitment and purpose to drive them toward success.

The first is that someone along the way convinced them that they had no purpose or that passion in business wasn't something they needed. As a result, people often gloss over sections in books like this in search of "the useful stuff."

I would suggest that if you do the exercises as described in this chapter, you will uncover a sense of purpose that can act as a tremendous source of energy to fuel your business and your life.

The key to making this concept work is belief. I find that if someone doesn't believe they'll find an answer to the question of their purpose in life, then they won't stay with it long enough to do so.

This idea of belief even plays out in things we may define as more scientific in nature.

In 1965, Intel cofounder Gordon Moore wrote an article noting a trend in microchips. His observation, popularly known as Moore's law, stated that the number of transistors on a chip will double approximately every two years.[*]

Moore's law is not really a law at all. It's an uncanny observation that some would suggest has driven the entire tech industry and remained true to prediction for over thirty years. There are those who also believe, like Moore, that the prediction merely became the

[*] Gordon E. Moore, "Cramming More Components onto Integrated Circuits," *Electronics* (1965), 4.

industry standard and scientists used it as the measure of competitiveness, creating a self-fulfilling prophecy.

Deeply felt passion, purpose, and intention have the same self-fulfilling power.

The other behavior that keeps people from tapping the incredible power of purpose is that they simply don't think big enough to create commitment.

My hope is that after you finish this chapter, you will be able to define your own personal sense of purpose in a way that both inspires and makes you nervous.

Build a bigger purpose and let it build a bigger you.

## What Our Fears Are Here to Tell Us

Before we move on to exercises designed to help build a bigger you, let me add one more thought about what might be holding you back.

One evening I was sitting around a dinner table with a number of colleagues. A couple of the folks were pretty engaged in a conversation about another speaker who was not present and suggested that he was a fraud.

The sentiment was that he didn't really know what he was talking about because he had never really done what it was he was advising people to do.

They eventually got around to asking me if I agreed and I said something like "Heck, we're all making it up, aren't we?" Now, that wasn't really what they wanted to hear, so after a polite laugh, they returned to the bashing.

What I really wanted to do was ask the woman who questioned me why she was so afraid that this person was succeeding. I wanted to suggest that maybe what she really feared was that people thought she was a fraud and that perhaps her deepest fear was that she would be found out if she didn't keep telling everyone that she was the real deal.

Don't get me wrong; at times, I myself do exactly what I'm suggesting this woman was doing. But I've come to understand the things that we judge, dislike, or criticize the most in others are probably a reflection of our own fears and insecurities.

As soon as we accept that about our own businesses, we'll start to experience a greater measure of peace. The competition is about being the best version of us and not about being a better version of someone else.

The key to embracing this way of thinking is to pay attention to times when we judge something as either good or bad and ask what that thought or feeling is really telling us about ourselves. When you become mindful of how much you're doing this, it will be eye-opening and maybe even a little humorous.

The thing is, we don't just do this with other people. We constantly do it to ourselves, and it's the source of most personal and business friction. For example:

**I'm not a good speaker.** Maybe you're not right now, but consider that we don't need you to be what you think is a good speaker. What we need you to be is a giver of information. Who are you not to do that?

**I hate to sell.** Maybe you hate to force something on somebody who doesn't want it, but consider that you have the opportunity to greatly impact someone's life by helping them understand the value that's contained in your product or lesson. Who are you not to do that?

**I could never charge that much.** There is no greater example of how our real fears and insecurities mask their existence than in the subject of value exchange. Are you charging less than you're worth? Who are you to do that?

What's holding you back now?

I believe that every one of us is powerful beyond belief and that our fears are actually signposts that mark the path we need to travel. Our fears are here to tell us what to do. Stop handling your fears and insecurities like baggage and start letting them act as your guide.

## Your Passion Mantra

By way of definition, a mantra is a sound, syllable, word, or group of words that is considered capable of "creating transformation." Its use and type varies according to the school and philosophy associated with the mantra.

I'm not using the term *mantra* in a religious context, but I use the idea of a mantra because I think it's a great business concept.

Throughout history, mantras were created and used as a centering tool or as a way to refocus a person's thinking on purpose.

I think everyone can benefit from creating their own unique personal mantra and use it as a trigger to snap them back into their best view of the world no matter what's going on.

I want to take you through a series of steps aimed at helping you create a personal statement or mantra that can become the reminder for your reason for doing what you do. You may or may not ever choose to share this mantra with anyone; simply possessing it makes it real.

In order to get the most from this exercise, you'll need a notebook, a blank sheet of paper, a word processor, or a note-keeping tool like Evernote.

I suggest that you set up and organize a system that allows you to access your notes throughout this journey and beyond. I've filled dozens of Moleskine notebooks by way of journaling over the years and I love going back over them. You'll find that purpose evolves as you grow. Having access to your ramblings in an archive is an important learning tool.

Get yourself and your notes in a place where you can focus uninterrupted for thirty minutes or so.

Now, at the top of your page, write the title **My Passion Mantra**.

Use about one-third of the page to answer each of the following questions. Write whatever comes to mind; don't judge, don't edit, just write. You might be surprised by some of the things that make your list, but it's important that you stay with it long enough to get past the first few obvious answers.

**1. What *do* you want in your life?** List the things, relationships, feelings, and experiences you know you want to have in your life, even if you don't have them right now.

**2. What *don't* you want in your life?** To some degree, this is merely the flip side of the first question, but many people can more readily define what they don't want than what they do want. You may find that you jump back and add some things to your first list after making this list.

The answers contained on both of the lists typically look like a list of your deeply held beliefs and values.

**3. What are you willing to give up in order to have what you want?** Taken in the right context, this is perhaps the hardest question anyone will ever ask you. On the surface it may appear that I'm asking you to identify things you are willing to sacrifice, like a car or vacation, but I'm not. This list is meant to be a list of the limiting behaviors, beliefs, and actions you might need to jettison in order to have the things you say you want in life.

For many people, it's this list that contains the secret to passion and purpose. We have the ability as human beings, either consciously or unconsciously, to build many of our own constraints. I have done this exercise privately with many business owners and this question often brings them to tears. Not because it's painful, but because it's freeing.

I once had a business owner do this exercise and he discovered that one thing that was holding him back from serving his life purpose was his nagging need to be right all the time. He discovered that this trait, perhaps something that had been with him since childhood, was keeping him from having rich relationships with his clients and his staff.

When he consciously began to let this need fall away, it changed everything and allowed him to live on purpose. That's the kind of discovery I hope you can make. Once you give yourself the permission and space to think bigger, you can start to analyze the things that need to change in order for it to be true.

Finally, we need to take the work you've done and start to develop a theme or mantra that will serve as the representation for what you want your life to mean. This isn't a laundry list of roles or things you want to accomplish, but a succinct and very repeatable (to yourself at least) statement of purpose.

Start another document and at the top of this one write: **My Passion-in-Life Mantra Is . . .**

Now take the most potent ingredients from the previous three questions and use them to help you answer the primary passion question.

You won't get it right the first time, so keep writing the answer over again. You probably won't get it right on the twentieth or thirtieth time, but keep writing. Write until you create something that literally takes your breath away. Not for its beauty or eloquence, but for the way it inspires you.

I wish I could share an example of a mantra here to demonstrate what this might look like, but my experience is that a list of mantras would only rob you of the ability to find something that truly moves you. There is no primary purpose mantra that is right or that sounds good and no element that should be in there. It simply must move you and it must inspire you.

If you stay with this exercise, I assure you something beautiful will emerge. I'm not precisely sure why this works, but I've never seen it fail.

# 4

# An Inside Job

**Contrary to how you might** be feeling at this point, discovering and recording a sense of passion and purpose and capturing a mantra that excites you is actually the easy part.

Staying connected to the words in that mantra, carrying it into every business situation, and using it as a filter for decision making—that's the hard part.

Staying committed to your purpose is the ultimate inside job, and as I'm sure you've already discovered at some point, you'll be tested frequently.

Your own fears, doubts, failures, and successes, not to mention a handful of hobbling ideas tossed in somewhere along the way by our well-intentioned parents and educators, will show up time and time again in the form of resistance and distraction.

Over the years I've developed a set of tools that I return to in an effort to maintain my own internal sense of who I am and how I intend for my business to serve.

This is not a comprehensive guide; it's simply an explanation of a few of the most powerful practices I attempt to maintain in an effort to support the balance my business is willing to rip apart.

## Business Is the Ultimate Adventure

At times, everything about running a business can feel very, very hard.

But here's something I've come to accept: everything in business and in life is driven by how we choose to view, accept, and react to the daily patterns and actions going on all around us.

There is a definable hard and easy, rigid and loose, ebb and flow that every business develops, and harmony comes from a place where this repetition and uncertainty collide.

Which is another way of saying that we can either choose to look at this business we've created as an awesome adventure or as a remarkable imposition, but make no mistake, it's simply a choice in how we view our life.

You can make your business fully alive by stuffing it with adventure and life or you can let it suck the life out of you, because frankly, it's capable of either.

For years I've relied on a simple thought to pull me along in those times when I don't feel like doing something I must, or when I wonder why I have to work harder than everyone else or why I'm not making as much money as some much more successful person. That mantra is: *My life is an amazing adventure; my business is an amazing adventure.*

Whenever I find my passion for some aspect of my business waning, I can simply trigger this thought, which helps me realign with the idea that everything I'm experiencing is simply part of the ride.

Don't let the simplicity of this idea escape you. Telling yourself you can't make it has just as much power over your ability to succeed as telling yourself you can.

See, that's the trickiest part. Not only is it an adventure, it's the adventure you've chosen. In moments of perfect silence and solitude, you can plainly see this, but when you are out in the world, you'll find it harder to live the adventure day to day. To truly live, however, is to embrace your own personal adventure in the midst of those who think they know your place better than you do.

So once you accept this notion that everything going on in your life and your business is as it should be, is part of the adventure you created, you are then free to choose a different adventure or a greater adventure if you like.

A greater adventure calls for more thinking, more acting, and most importantly, more acceptance that everything going on is simply part of the ride.

I'm not going to submit that there aren't truly rough patches in owning a business, but I do know that you can find some peace, even in the roughest patches, when you accept that you're simply on the adventure you signed up for.

## How to Be Present for Your Business

The ability, some might say the attempt, to multitask is a curse of sorts. While working on ten things at once may seem efficient, each of those things gets roughly 10 percent of our greatness while we're doing it.

That may actually be fine for, say, deleting e-mails, but is it enough for writing a note to a client, creating an action plan for a product launch, or determining the fee you plan to charge for a project? Probably not.

Attention is one of our scarcest resources these days, and guarding it in a way that allows us to work with intention requires the ability to remain present and mindful in the midst of the storm raging all around us. (Otherwise known as your business.)

In fact, the ability to work with intention requires us not only to be as present as possible for the daily tasks we tackle, but also to be continually mindful of where we are going and why we are going there, and that requires a process of its own.

### Planned Mindfulness

It's one thing to conduct annual strategic planning sessions and quite another to live the intention of those sessions after the whiteboards are erased.

I believe that you need to create a daily routine that involves revisiting your greatest goals and objectives and developing a passion mantra that upon seeing, hearing, or reading energizes you and snaps you back into a state of mindfulness.

## Witness Your Thoughts

Another habit that you may need to form in order to work steadily toward the goals of your business is to start to pay attention to your thoughts and reactions throughout the day.

Frankly, this can be exhausting work, but if you can begin to step back and analyze how your mind unconsciously processes everything that happens throughout the day, you might start to get a glimpse into some of the negative and limiting ways we view things as either good or bad.

The problem with most of our reactions is that they don't always serve our overall objectives. If your intention is to be a business that provides incredible value by helping your customers achieve their goals, you'll find that giving more than you take is the surest path to success. However, if your first thought in most relationships is *What's in it for me?* or *I've got to watch my back,* you've got some powerful forces working against you.

How we view things is simply a choice, but that choice can become so ingrained that it occurs out of habit. When we start to slow down and observe these choices as they are happening, we gain the power to make them or not according to our intentions.

## Be Present

Our intentions drive our thoughts and our thoughts form our actions. That's what makes planning, goal setting, and mindful thinking so powerful.

In addition to witnessing how your thoughts create and form your reality, you must develop habits that help you change your physical state and bring it intentionally into the present.

This is the easy part. Develop routines that require you to stop your work hourly and do ten push-ups or take a lap around your office building. Fill up a jug of water and empty it hourly. Take a fifteen-minute afternoon nap. Write a handwritten thank-you note several times a day.

What you do physically isn't as important as the act of stopping and bringing your awareness back into the room by removing your attention from all the tasks at hand. I find that the simplest acts of planned physical mindfulness, even intentional breathing, have the power to center me.

## Be Present for Customers

The point of all of this mindfulness is to help you build a better business that delivers value to the world and less stress to you in the process. The practical side is that you will be present for your customers, which will lead to an immediate payoff.

We all like to think we have our customers' needs and desires in mind at all times, but we often get caught up in appearing to have all the answers, in pushing our agendas rather than listening, or in feigning care when our real motivation is the sale.

You can't be fully present in every client interaction, but occasionally, maybe systematically, you need to look your clients in the eye, in a way that lets them feel you are listening, and ask them how you could help them more—and then shut up and listen without judgment. My guess is you will find this to be incredibly rewarding.

## Be Present for Staff

In the midst of the day-to-day rush of projects, tasks, questions, and actions, the development of the people who work around you can get lost.

Meetings are scheduled and conducted with to-dos and takeaways in mind and are often seen as a roadblock to getting your real work done.

Again, you can't be fully mindful in every interaction with your staff, but in order to create an environment where your people can participate in the fulfillment of the organization's objectives, you must provide a way for them to be heard as well.

Once a week, put thirty minutes on your calendar with everyone who reports to you and make them own the agenda. There may be times when several agenda items revolve around projects, but there will be other times when you simply listen to their descriptions of what they really want out of life and consider how you can help them get there. I believe that may be one of the most rewarding gifts you can give.

This "being present" stuff isn't for the timid, but if you've ever come home at night and couldn't really tell your spouse what you did all day that made you so busy, there's a pretty good bet you need to dig into this.

## The Business Case for Solitude

One of the things business owners don't get enough of is solitude. We are constantly surrounded by coworkers, prospects, suppliers, and customers in a never-ending battle to grow the business.

Don't get me wrong, plenty of business owners operate on their own, but solitude and loneliness are not the same thing.

Solitude is an intentional step away from every possible distraction. Even folks who work alone suffer from the constant pull of e-mail, phone calls, and dozens of online social interactions and distractions.

In order to stay true to your business and purpose you must explore ways to create intentional solitude or what I like to call the *solo planning practice.*

John Ratliff, owner of Appletree Answers, takes a full three days each year and goes by himself to a cabin to get his thoughts for the year down on paper. He emerges with pages and pages of notes that become the framework for the strategic planning meetings he holds with his leadership team during the year.

He claims it is both the hardest and most fruitful thing he does each year.

The idea behind any practice is the act of doing something habitually or repetitively in the hope of getting better at it. There are countless patterns and actions that business owners do almost daily that certainly meet the definition of practice; selling, writing, speaking, training, educating, and documenting are just a few.

When you add the systematic practice of solitude to this list, you may gain greater access to the following business and life benefits and find that you can more easily keep your business purpose in line with your life purpose.

**Hear yourself.** A business can create so much noise that it becomes hard to listen to your own guiding voice. When we react, without witnessing our thoughts and actions through our true voice, we set ourselves up to be influenced in ways that are not authentic. Have you ever found yourself doing or saying something, and soon after found yourself thinking, *That's not me, that's not how I want my business to run?*

The voice in your head, the one that tells you why you're doing what you're doing, who you are, and how you want others to experience you, is your true voice speaking with purpose, and solitude is the way you let that voice come back and remind you why you do what you do. This voice refuses to shout over the noise and deserves your full attention.

**Get clarity.** Once you return to hearing yourself, you can begin to organize what that means. Have you ever had one of those times when things don't make sense and you don't feel like you can find an answer? Or worse, things just don't seem like fun anymore. Then, seemingly out of nowhere, a simple, elegant, perfect answer presents itself. That's one of the things that being alone with your thoughts can offer. You get the chance to relax and not try to find or force answers, which is, of course, what makes them appear.

Clarity is what you need in order to make the big decisions about your business, about your people, and about the marketplace. Without it, you'll be driven by the rush of the day and idea of the week.

**Learn to speak.** Sometimes I talk too much. Most of us do. We get very nervous when there is silence and we stretch to fill up the silence whether it needs us to or not. This is as true for the stammering we do in front of a prospect as it is for the conversations we have with ourselves. One of the odd benefits of the practice of solitude is that it better prepares us to not say anything, to have the confidence that just enough has been said about something or someone, and to know when to ask for help, when to say no, and when to stand firm.

This, of course, can transfer over into our writing as well.

**Keep evolving.** Innovation and creativity in most small businesses develop in layers. It's very difficult to come up with an idea for a service or product that won't impact the overall brand, strategy, culture, and customer.

Quite often we get what seems like a great idea and we lurch into full implementation mode.

By stepping into solitude and summoning your thoughts about your business, you are more likely to start at the necessary level to consider the strategic impact first and, from there, more accurately develop the projects, actions, patterns, and processes needed to bring your innovation to life.

**Renew purpose.** As I've already stated in this book, I believe that one of the greatest reasons to create a business is to create purpose, purpose in your life, in the lives of those who work with you, and at some level, in the lives of those who experience the business as customers, suppliers, and mentors.

Practicing solitude forces you to consider, evaluate, and connect with that purpose even as the constant natural forces of business try to erode it.

This is what turns simple passion into focused commitment. Don't wait until you go on vacation to consider this idea. Instead, make it part of the game, build it into the culture of your business, and teach your customers about silence and solitude as an essential aspect of your brand.

Decide what your intentional solo planning practice is going to look like. Is it an hour a week or an entire day once a quarter? Can you pair it with another passion such as painting or a walk in the woods? Can you start small and build to the point where it captures a significant amount of your attention?

## How to Be Really, Really Good at Everything You Do

When it comes to excelling at running a business, the common advice among experts is to identify your strengths and weaknesses and build on things you're good at while finding ways to shore up your weaknesses.

I have a different view. I think society and our past experiences can mask our real strengths and trick us into focusing on the wrong things entirely.

People who have been led to the accounting industry, for example, in some cases because they couldn't decide on anything else to study in school, are often told that their lack of creativity is a weakness.

Artists are made to believe that making a profit or organizing a business that allows them to mass-personalize their art makes them a sellout or worse.

Simply having experience doing a certain kind of work is not necessarily the same as having a special talent or knack for a certain kind of work.

I think business owners need to find and tap their superpower and then apply it to every aspect of their business.

Here's what I mean: while some might look at me and suggest my strengths are writing and speaking, they would miss my superpower, which is curiosity.

The reason my business exists is that I want to know how things work and why. I want to know what makes people tick. I want to know how to do everything in a new and original way.

When I'm faced with doing something I don't know how to do or something I know I need to permit myself to do, I don't try to figure out how everyone else has done it. Instead, I engage my curiosity in how it's done, and I turn it into something I can explore and take part in. That is what gets me by.

This view allows me to be fearless in my approach to almost anything I do, no matter what the task at hand.

I have seven brothers and two sisters and my parents would always joke that when we were little and they took the ten of us on some adventure (any trip is an adventure with ten kids), their strategy was to divide and conquer, which meant Dad would watch me and Mom would watch the other nine. My superpower found me at an early age.

Do you know your superpower? Everyone has at least one, and if you can find a way to bring it to work in every aspect of the day, you'll develop a powerful supercharged business-building tool.

Is it insight, caring, math, vision, listening, hustle, flow, calmness, persistence, or, perhaps, curiosity?

You may have to dig deep to reacquaint yourself with it. You may have masked it because you think it's not very business-oriented. You may have to go back to when you thought anything was possible, back to when you played like a kid.

Go back and look at the exercise where you listed what you want and don't want in your life. Do those lists hold any clues to your superpower?

Finding and using your superpower is like tuning in to a potent frequency. It's a fearless, never-fail instinct that can inform every decision you make about your business. If you lose this signal, if fear creeps in, your passion for your business will drain. Guard your superpower wisely.

Your superpower is your greatest defender; it shreds resistance and that inner and outer critic that tells you something is hard and that you're no good at it, so why bother.

Your superpower helps you tune out those invested in keeping you right where you are.

Your superpower zaps fear.

## "If This, Then That" Thinking

Reaching your goals takes hard work, drive, and, more than anything, consistent action that moves you in the direction of your goals.

One of the challenges to your ability to take the right action is habits or lack of them. Our habits either take us where we want to go or hold us back perpetually. Everyone operates this way. Millionaires and drug addicts are both driven by habits; they are just different habits.

Once you determine the actions you must take in order to move toward your dreams, you must get in the habit of taking those actions routinely.

While doing some of my habitual Web surfing, digging and discovering, I recently came across a Web app called If This Then That, or IFTTT.com. The idea behind the service is pure genius and in my opinion a tool that you should check out.

IFTTT.com helps you automate tasks that might make your online life easier and more efficient. The idea behind an IFTTT formula is that you define a trigger—such as "If I post to Twitter"—and then define a supplemental action—such as "then send a copy to Evernote."

With this conditional statement in place (of course you have to provide access to both your Twitter and Evernote accounts), you can automatically create a note in Evernote that keeps a record of every one of your Tweets.

The creative possibilities of this type of conditional statement writing are mind-boggling once you start to think about it.

Remember how I started off by talking about creating habits that move you toward your goals?

As I played around with this trigger-and-action thinking, it dawned on me that I've been using this concept for years in my own habit formation and you can use it as well to reinforce actions that you need to take.

If there's an action that you know you need to take routinely, the trick to doing it more consistently and perhaps even making it a bit more fun to do is to connect a trigger to its achievement.

I believe you can use this for the simplest of tasks and even for more time-consuming, mentally and physically challenging actions. In fact, you can even use this conditional thinking to turn habit formation into a game.

Here's a very simple example that helps me stay focused on a very positive business routine. Each day I am committed to writing five handwritten notes. So that I won't forget, I've set up a rule that says that once I complete a phone call, I have to write a note thanking a client.

I know this is a pretty simple example, but I think it might help you start to see the logic behind the concept and how applying this logic to many areas could help you keep the focus on positive habit development.

## Give Yourself Permission to Fail

When I was growing up, I decided I wanted to play the guitar. I loved music, appreciated songwriting, and wanted to be able to play and sing. As anyone who has ever tried to learn an instrument or anyone who's lived with someone trying to learn a musical instrument can attest, at first you're going to be really, really bad.

But, if your desire to play is strong and you push through with practice, eventually something magical can occur. Now, I never practiced enough to expect to rise very high in my musical career, but I did advance to the point where I could earn money, tips, and drinks by playing in the bars in the town where I attended college. (I'm convinced this helped me attract my wife too.)

If you want to achieve any level of success in your business, one of the things you must do is give yourself permission to be bad at the things you don't know how to do.

You grow the most when you make mistakes, and when you're not comfortable. I'm not wishing for hard times to visit, but I do know that historically some of the greatest business breakthroughs happen when we are dead wrong in our assumptions and fall flat on our face, but have the guts to get up and figure out what we just learned.

I frequently encounter business owners who tell me they are bad at this or that or they fear they can't master an important skill. The thing about holding back or caving in to fear is that it zaps your passion and kills your commitment.

There are so many things you must do in order to build a business and in most cases you'll have no idea how to do them properly and no experience to draw upon other than what you witness around you. Many business owners plainly ignore some of the steps they must take in order to move their business forward with momentum because they don't think they know enough about how to do something, or they don't think they like that kind of work, or someone told them they're no good at something.

If you've ever felt like your business is stuck and you keep bumping up against some unseen force that won't let you move forward, look no further than yourself. The enemy is you and your unwillingness to do the things you must do even though you're afraid you'll fail.

There's a chapter in the wonderful book *Bird by Bird* by Anne Lamott titled "Shitty First Drafts." Lamott describes a process of writing that involves getting something down on paper, without analysis, knowing that it won't be very good, but also knowing that it's the only way to get to the second and final draft. Unless you're willing to write something very badly, you'll never get to something beautiful.*

When I realized that in order to build the business I wanted to build I would have to write every day, I just started to write. I had never really written this way and I wasn't very good. I didn't want to be bad at it, but I gave myself permission to suck because it was the only way I was going to get where I wanted to go.

When I realized that in order to build the business I wanted to build I would have to get up in front of audiences and speak, I just started to do it. I had never done it before and I wasn't very good. I didn't want to be bad at it, but I gave myself permission to suck because it was the only way I was going to get somewhere I wanted to go.

I'm by no means a great writer or a great speaker, but I've stuck with both long enough to get to the point where they've become essential elements of my business and brand because I knew they had to be.

---

* Anne Lamott, *Bird by Bird: Some Instructions on Writing and Life* (New York: Anchor, 1995).

Give yourself permission to be bad at doing the things you want and need to do and you might find that your art flows more easily.

## The Math of Energy

Small-business ownership is hard work. Physically demanding, stressful, mind-numbing work—and that's on the good days. But, like you, I wouldn't trade it for the world. One of the benefits of owning a small business is that you are free—free to work any eighty hours a week you choose, right?

But no matter how efficient you are, there's always more to do than there is time to do it.

That's the number one complaint I hear from small-business owners: I just don't have enough time to do it all.

For me, one of the secrets to getting more time each day is to pay attention to my physical energy and do everything I can to enhance, store, and build it.

Spending time engaged in daily exercise is an example of an energy-building practice that actually gives me time instead of costing time.

Some of what eventually turned into my greatest innovations and ideas simply came to me during an early-morning run in the neighborhood.

- I started running for exercise in high school and it's one of the most relaxing forms of energy creation for me.
- Conscious eating, whatever that might mean to you, is another energy-building practice.
- Meditation and yoga are two powerful forms of stress reduction and energy building.
- White-noise generator Simply Noise allows me to tune out distractions and gain instant focus.
- Spending time in nature allows me to reconnect with my body's natural rhythm.

- Reading lyrical passages of literature such as those found in *Anam Cara* by John O'Donohue is energy and focus building.*
- Creating boundaries by shutting down all the technology in my life for periods of time and calming the need to respond to every e-mail request is an energy-building practice.

These are just some of the practices I keep in the energy toolbox. I know you didn't buy this book looking for a lesson on healthy living, but it's very hard to disconnect the physical you from the creative you.

There's a terrific book by Jim Loehr and Tony Schwartz called *The Power of Full Engagement* that covers this topic in a very specific way. Loehr and Schwartz started working with elite athletes in an effort to help them manage their energy to enhance their performance.†

When they took their discoveries to the world of business, they made this unexpected observation: "The performance demands that most people face in their everyday work environments dwarf those of any professional athlete we have ever trained."

I suspect everyone knows they can take better care of their physical selves, particularly as they get older, but I wonder if you've considered the role this kind of commitment to energy building could play in helping you deliver purpose, maintain focus, and bring only the healthiest emotions to the game.

I know that every single day that I get some exercise, I get more done. Mind you, I don't exercise enough, but I can tell you that investing 30 of the 1,440 minutes I have in a day in energy-building activities always pays off in terms of increased productivity.

Go out and get a personal trainer, invest in a chef, create technology boundaries, start learning as much as you can about keeping

---

* John O'Donohue, *Anam Cara: A Book of Celtic Wisdom* (New York: HarperCollins, 1997).
† Jim Loehr and Tony Schwartz, *The Power of Full Engagement* (New York: Simon & Schuster, 2003).

your body and mind well. It's one of the best investments you can make in your business and your purpose.

## How to Think Differently

One of the greatest constraints that business owners face is the inability to view things from a different perspective. Continuing to return to a business with the same ideas and experiences of our past or our industry norm is what makes innovation, growth, and creativity seem so hard.

Being well versed in your industry is essential, but it can also cripple creative thinking.

One of the ways to stoke your creativity and think about challenges and opportunities differently is to consume a diet of writing and thinking from other fields.

Great artists and other creatives are often blessed with the gift, or curse as it may be, of seeing things in a new way, seeing negative space as the real potential, or finding patterns in nature and culture that give way to discoveries in seemingly unrelated fields.

While the traditionally analytical business owner may not view himself as naturally creative, a new view can be acquired if he's open to it.

One of my favorite ways to gain access to other fields is to view TED Talks online. These short presentations, given by inspirational leaders from all walks of life, are like little snack-size innovation bursts. The speakers often focus on one very specific idea and the format calls for both brevity and simplicity. It's the perfect recipe to change your view of your business or industry.

Below are five books that I turn to, to help me find ways to unlock new business perspectives, precisely because they are not business books.

*The Timeless Way of Building* by Christopher Alexander. This classic explains the idea of patterns in architecture. While architects are very familiar with this work, I am always blown away by the practical application of this one idea: a pattern is a way to solve a specific problem, by bringing two conflicting forces into balance. I think the study of patterns is such a fascinating way to view business, selling, systems, and customers.

*The Calculus Diaries: How Math Can Help You Lose Weight, Win in Vegas, and Survive a Zombie Apocalypse* by Jennifer Ouellette. *The Calculus Diaries* is the fun and fascinating account of English major Jennifer Ouellette's year spent confronting her math phobia head-on. With a fair amount of humor tossed in, Ouellette shows how she learned to apply calculus to everything from gas mileage to dieting, from the rides at Disneyland to shooting craps in Vegas—proving that even the mathematically challenged can learn the fundamentals of the universal language. I don't recommend this book because I want you to learn calculus. I think this book demonstrates how you can totally change your view of something when you start to look for practical applications. So many people can relate to math phobia and I think there are many business phobias that need a new look as well.

*Envisioning Information* by Edward Tufte. This is a visually gorgeous book that you might find on a coffee table, but it's not just to flip through. This is a book that you need to spend time with, as it presents the best examples of visual information design and the underlying principles that make great design work so well. It's easy to see how this book should be required reading for any Web-page designer, UI designer, statistician, cartographer, or scientist, but today every business owner must be concerned with presenting dense information in a clear way, and this book lets you see how to do just that.

*The Ramen King and I: How the Inventor of Instant Noodles Fixed My Love Life* by Andy Raskin. Anyone who has the nerve to jump into this entire list may find this book to be both the most entertaining and oddest. This autobiography by NPR commentator Andy Raskin is humorous, odd, and spiritual. For me, the best part was an introduction to the Japanese art of sushi making, which is a wonderful, patient art. In the end, Raskin realizes that in order to quell his demons, he is going to have to face them and reassess how he looks at his life, a lesson for many a business owner.

*The Art of Learning: An Inner Journey to Optimal Performance* by Josh Waitzkin. Waitzkin is a world champion chess player and subject of the 1993 movie *Searching for Bobby Fischer*. In this memoir, he reveals how his skill with chess can be applied to the seemingly much more physically demanding sport of tai chi. He took the sport up in an effort to experience that process of learning something new and had no intention of competing, and became a champion. In *The Art of Learning*, he shares how anyone can learn how to tap new perspectives to create optimal performance.

I hope you enjoyed this tour of some of my best tools for holding on to and cherishing purpose. Now it's your turn to develop your tool set by adopting, adapting, and adding to the list.

# 5

# The Purpose of a Business

**Up to this point, I've** used the words *passion* and *purpose* in the context of your life's purpose. Now I want to shift the focus to the purpose of your business. These are two distinct, yet intrinsically intertwined ideas.

Peter Drucker wrote in *The Practice of Management* that "the purpose of a business is to create and keep a customer."*

While that may indeed be true, it's the bare minimum and something that's required to keep the doors open unless you're funded by a venture capitalist. To aim just to create and keep a customer, as the purpose of a business, is to shoot terribly low.

> **I believe the purpose of a business is to create and keep purpose.**

While a purpose related to business can be a loaded concept for some, I think that in this day and age businesses that are built to do something that people can rally around, regardless of what the

---

* Peter F. Drucker, *The Practice of Management* (New York: Harper & Row, 1954), 12.

company actually makes and sells, are the ones that will naturally experience commitment and growth.

Organizations that can foster and communicate what I call throughout this book a "higher purpose," will always attract employees, customers, and opportunities that are drawn to that higher purpose. This is also a great way to maintain focus in business.

Some of the most successful brands today—including Apple, Zappos, and Southwest, to name a few—have captured people's hearts and imaginations through a simple purpose. A purpose doesn't always have to be a noble cause. Purpose can be an innovation or an ideal like great service or design, a culture built around fun, or a single idea like trust.

People commit to companies, products, and stories that are built on and positioned with a simple, easy-to-communicate purpose. We commit to things we believe in and companies that understand this make their entire marketing about purpose instead of product.

- 37signals is an antisoftware company that happens to make the simplest software on the planet.
- Evernote has built universal trust through data by creating a place to store and file things you want to remember.
- Zappos is built around happiness yet they sell shoes and clothes.
- Southwest Airlines has fun while making travel less costly and less of a hassle.
- Apple makes computers for people who want a simple, intuitive, and stunningly designed experience.

I propose that commitment to a product, service, company, or job is rooted in making a personal connection, and connection comes from building a business around a single-minded purpose that happens to sell something.

What does this mean for your business? Can you discover a purpose greater than simply creating a customer? Can you create a business and a culture that communicates that purpose? What might change if you did? What organizations could you model your purpose on? How can you draw people to commit and connect to your higher purpose?

# The Alchemy of Purpose

Where your talents and the needs of the world intersect, there lies your calling.

—*Aristotle*

Alchemy was a form of chemistry and speculative philosophy practiced in the Middle Ages and the Renaissance; it was concerned principally with discovering methods for changing metals into gold and with finding the elixir of life.

The efforts of the original alchemists were considered unsuccessful, as they never produced gold. But they are credited with aiding in the development of modern pharmacy, chemistry, and medicine.

I think the idea of generating purpose has a great deal in common with the notion of alchemy. We start with a handful of ingredients, and in an effort to produce gold, we end up discovering the real manner in which we are destined to make a difference.

So far, most of the work on the idea of purpose has centered on the personal and unique you, the life focus. Now let's take what we've done so far and shine the light of purpose on your work life or business.

The objective of this chapter is to help you assemble the words, tools, and tactics that you will use to inject a single-minded driving sense of higher purpose into your overall business strategy.

Of course, words without consistent actions are meaningless, but the first step is to build the emotion around the words in ways that motivate you to think and act on purpose.

I'm going to ask you to once again grab your notebook or computer and make a couple more lists in response to the questions below.

## 1. What do you love most about your work?

Make a list of all the things that you do in your work that you truly enjoy. Don't hold back, and list whatever comes to mind. These are the kinds of things that you find yourself thinking you might do even if no one paid you to do them. They are the kinds of things you stick with because you enjoy doing them, even though the payoff may never happen.

When I first started blogging, it was completely a labor of love. I wanted to write more and I knew producing good content would allow me to build a following, but in the beginning it was simply work that I enjoyed doing.

It's important that in addition to making your list, you take some time and try to understand why you enjoy certain kinds of work. To the right of each entry on your list, include a little note that describes what you get out of doing that work or why it engages you.

## 2. Whom do you want to see you as a hero?

To me, this is the money question because it causes you to think about what you do in much bigger terms. Sure the word *hero* might hold comic-book or overly dramatic connotations when you think about applying it to yourself or your business, but it's a crucial part of making the connection to purpose.

True leadership involves creating and telling stories that generate commitment and inspire action in others, but the first story is the one you tell yourself. Painting the picture of yourself in the role of the leader is your most important story.

I'm not talking about trying to be some sort of self-appointed torchbearer. I'm simply suggesting that you need to have a clear picture of the people you want to impact most. By making this decision, you are equipped to accomplish the real job of a leader: to help others view themselves as heroes in their own story.

When you understand that the ultimate role of a leader is to inspire others, there is a far greater chance that you will make the right decisions.

In an effort to get even more perspective around this idea, consider this question: who are your heroes? You don't have to use the word *hero*. I use it here for impact, but you could just as easily substitute *admire, respect,* and *look up to.*

This is how you connect what your business does with why your business does it and whom it does it for.

Whether we realize it or not, storytelling is an essential activity of human beings, and heroes are an essential element in every story. We are told stories from the time we are able to comprehend them until the time we leave this world. It's how we create meaning; it's how we construct and deconstruct the world we live in. Stories move us to action and inspire us to think bigger.

There is a classic book written by Joseph Campbell called *The Hero with a Thousand Faces.* This work, a study of comparative mythology, is a must-read for business owners and marketers, as it reveals the entire road map for the power of stories throughout time.*

## 3. How can this business serve your passion?

This is the all-important bridge between your personal passion and your business purpose.

Patton Gleason is a runner who became totally immersed in the practice and art of running. He wondered why most sports practices focused a tremendous amount of energy on learning the fundamentals of the sport, the form, the physiology, while runners simply went out and trained.

---

* Joseph Campbell, *The Hero with a Thousand Faces* (Princeton, N.J.: Princeton University Press, 1968).

Gleason is the owner of NaturalRunningStore.com, a company that specializes in providing minimalist shoes and gear. Ask most of their customers and they'll tell you they are drawn to Gleason's passion for a better way of running.

Gleason told me that when he got started with this idea, "I wondered if I could understand the things that make people happiest and bring those same attributes to running with the idea that the happiest runner was the best runner. At first, I just started studying this idea out of curiosity really."

This study turned into something he called the Flow Running Project.

"Making happy runners and helping people understand that their bodies are perfect is deeply rooted in my personal passion and purpose," he says.

He took that personal drive and turned it into a business that teaches, inspires, and trains individuals to be happier, healthier, more natural runners. He also sells lots of shoes to people who are attracted to his message and his passion.

He's simply serving a purpose he's passionate about and in return he's a hero to a whole group of people. His "why" is so strong and authentic that people are drawn to do business with his company.

There is a particularly powerful passage in *Anam Cara* where the author talks about the idea that while the world has much for us to experience, most people stay locked up in a tower looking out only one window. And yet, real growth comes only from experiencing the view from all the windows.

"Complacency, habit and blindness often prevent you from feeling your life. So much depends on the frame of vision—the window through which you look."*

Shine a light and open some windows—that's the path I'm inviting you to follow.

---

* O'Donohue, *Anam Cara*, 127.

# Turning Purpose into Strategy

The final piece in the puzzle is to take the answers to the questions above and plug them into the ultimate strategy question for the fully alive business:

**How can you connect the elements of your personal purpose with a purpose for your business?**

Stop right now and think about the question above. Is there an answer you need to record in your notebook? Did you get a sense, perhaps for the first time, of the true nature of what drives you? Did this question give you the feeling of freedom that's been so hard to express up to now? Are you beginning to develop some clarity about the connection between your inner passion and outward action?

In the next chapter we will examine the issue of strategy meeting purpose and fill it with the seven characteristics of real-life strategy.

First, let me give you a few more thoughts on purpose.

If you stared into the Ultimate Strategy Question above and found that it didn't spark enough in you, don't panic. Let's just do a little more work using some techniques I've used over the years.

## Don't Try So Hard

Working on something as important as discovering your life mission can induce a great deal of stress and anxiety, but I've also seen it create a tremendous amount of joy.

You don't create revolutionary change and innovation by sitting down and trying to think it up. It doesn't work that way. It comes to you, from a place you can't really define, when you're not really thinking about it.

It's there, in the subconscious somewhere, and your job is to plant the seed and let it grow. Maybe you need to put this book down, sleep on it, and come back and see how it feels tomorrow.

Have you ever tried to remember some fact, like a name of someone from your past, and no matter how hard you tried, you just couldn't squeeze it out of your brain? Then, five minutes later, after you had given up trying, it simply came to you? Discovering your purpose and linking it to your business can be like that as well.

Here's a suggestion: close your eyes, relax, and think about the last time you really smiled about something in your business.

What was it about that moment that made you smile? What did you experience? What triggered that emotion? I call these *passion moments*. There is an element of purpose in passion moments and they can possess the answer to the question of how you're meant to serve.

## Paint an Image

Another effective way to think about purpose is to picture your future.

Dan Sullivan, creator of the Strategic Coach Program, has a wonderfully powerful question that he's posed to countless individuals seeking mission, vision, and purpose: "If we were having this discussion three years from today, and you were looking back over those three years, what has to happen in your life, personally and professionally, for you to feel happy with your progress?"

It's such a great question because it immediately forces you to create a picture of the future.

Now, while you start to fill in the elements of the picture, let me immediately ask you to think about another picture. What does your future look like if you fail to do anything, or worse, don't seize the opportunity to live with purpose? What does the worst-case scenario look like?

Contrast that picture with the one that makes you smile and you just might start to think bigger.

## Purpose Through Failure

What did you learn the last time something really flopped in your business?

I know it's a cliché to suggest that we learn most from our failures, but there's some truth to the notion. However, most people miss the point. It's not that you learn anything at all from failure itself; it's that you learn a lot about yourself and what you stand for by how you react to it.

I want you to focus all of your thinking on a moment of failure and the precise moment when you said to yourself, *Well, here's what we're going to do about it*. Re-create that feeling and you'll have a window into most everything that is true about you and your values.

Now let's connect the work you've done so far with strategy—real-life strategy, that is.

# 6

# Every Business Is a Marketing Business

**I believe that brilliant business** strategy is simply brilliant marketing strategy; as the chapter title states, every business is a marketing business. I know there are plenty of people who might debate that last statement, claiming there is a significant difference between the two ideas.

My contention is that anything a business does that impacts any member of the community surrounding the business—staff, vendors, customers, investors—is a marketing function.

In this chapter we are going to build on the purpose work you've done to this point and use it to help define your **Real-Life Marketing Strategy**. I use the term *real life* to refer to your marketing strategy because unlike most discussions about strategy, I'm talking about positioning with personality and implementing characteristics that you can see and feel and experience. Just like the search for purpose, your marketing strategy will be based on common human desires and aspirations.

# Your Real-Life Strategy

I've spent a great deal of time wrestling with the idea of developing
useful, real-life marketing strategies for small businesses and have
concluded that there are a handful of characteristics that can be
mined, explored, and shaped in order to make marketing strategy
the foundation of building a business.

As you may have surmised by this point, I believe that the key to
discovering an effective marketing strategy lies in understanding first
that its essence is much more about why a business does something
than about what or how the business does something.

What follows is an exploration of marketing strategy in the most
practical sense of the concept.

## Find a Single-Minded Strategy

I believe the most effective marketing strategies are held together
by getting really clear about one simple thing.

Bill Caskey, founder of Caskey Sales Training, a sales and leadership training and coaching firm in Indianapolis, describes his single-
minded discovery like this:

"When we first started I thought it was all about teaching people
how to be better at selling, but the more we got into it, I realized that
what we're about was bringing out the best in people. When we understood that, it changed everything. We moved away from selling and
started to focus on mental makeup, and it dramatically impacted our
business growth and success."

In many ways, this idea was born years before Caskey started his
own sales training business. As a junior salesperson for a large tool
manufacturer, he recalled one of his first sales presentations.

"I was in Nashville trying to close a very small sale and I recall how
nervous I was about making this pitch and ultimately how bad I was
at doing it. I vowed that day to do everything I could to get better at

this business, but struggled to find what I thought was any good information on professional selling."

So Caskey Sales Training was born out of his own pain and struggle to develop a skill that he knew was vital to many struggling with the same pain.

Countless organizations, just like Caskey Sales Training, have accomplished many things first and foremost through the realization of one single-minded purpose as their strategy. This single-minded purpose is the standard for every business decision, hiring decision, product decision, and marketing campaign. It often starts with the *here's-what-we-really-stand-for moment.*

Of course, finding and committing to a real-life marketing strategy isn't enough. You've also got to find a way to make it part of the DNA of the organization. You've got to find symbols and stories and metaphors that invite and allow every part of your business ecosystem to embrace the strategy.

## Now Express It

The most powerful form of value proposition for the fully alive business is the expression of a higher purpose in a way that allows people who share these beliefs to connect with your products.

Many texts on the subject talk about the idea of creating a value proposition by being the first to do something, the only one to package or ship a certain way, or by positioning your business against some standard practice in an industry.

While I believe it's important to understand what the market lacks and how your competition positions do what they do, it's more important to understand how to deliver purpose through how you do what you do.

Companies that focus on a proposition based on a product, service, or unique way of doing business are locked into that category and easily duplicated. Organizations that brand on purpose spend far less time being concerned with competition because it's impossible to copy purpose—purpose is DNA.

Organizations that focus on purpose, or why they do what they do, are often able to enter complementary markets much more easily because the association they carry into that market is based on purpose rather than product.

69

Your core message must be first and foremost about why the business does what it does and not about some way to position the products and services as the main act.

Leading with purpose is how your business communicates. If your purpose is why you do what you do, then your core message is how you deliver on this in a way that matters to your market.

One of best examples of this is shoe and apparel retailer Zappos. Zappos is often cited as a company that focuses on customer happiness and just happens to sell shoes. Zappos is rapidly entering other highly competitive markets based on their "why" more than anything else.

The creation of a brand or value proposition that also happens to represent your core beliefs is a tricky thing. The first rule, of course, should always be simplicity. Trying to explain everything your business stands for in every conceivable way is a recipe for confusion.

In fact, the kind of core message I'm talking about is one that can be summed up in one or two words. This is such an important concept to grasp because far too often business owners suffer from trying to communicate too much.

You've heard the expression "A picture is worth a thousand words." Well, the right one or two words are often worth more than ten thousand words.

To return to my earlier example of 37signals, you don't have to look much further than the tagline on the company's Web site to start to get a sense of how they position their sense of purpose in a way that allows the market to experience it:

"Making collaboration productive and enjoyable for people every day. Frustration-free Web-based apps for collaboration, sharing information, and making decisions."

The hunt for your one or two words starts with understanding where you stand right now.

If you've been in business for any time at all, there's a good chance you've already captured a place in the mind of your customers or market, but you just don't know it. In working with small businesses over the years, I've uncovered stunning differentiation strategies by simply going out and interviewing a handful of an organization's most loyal customers.

Customers often appreciate the little things you do differently: the fact that you care enough to clean up the job site each day, that you explain accounting in plain English, return phone calls promptly, or provide recommendations of other service providers. These are the kinds of things that demonstrate what you believe.

This is how your customers experience your purpose in action. In many cases, you don't see it as a strategy because you suspect it's how everyone runs their business.

The key is to find these little differentiators and make them a part of your core marketing message. Sometimes this takes guts. Maybe nobody else in your industry is promoting those little things and maybe they don't sound that sexy, but your best customers told you that they make a big difference to them and that should give you the confidence that it will make a big difference to others.

When you start with telling people why you do what you do, you won't have to revolutionize a product or service category to be different in ways that matter to your customers. You just have to innovate in ways that make sense to them and make your brand easy to talk about. Sometimes simplifying what you do can be the greatest innovation of all.

## Finding Your Value Proposition Message

Since one of the best ways to create positioning and messages that support your higher purpose is to start gathering themes and data on how your customers currently experience your business and your brand, it's a good idea to go out and interview your customers.

There's a good chance they can provide some clues to the actual words and phrases you need to adopt as your value proposition message. The great thing about building a brand founded on a higher purpose is that it allows people to connect based on their values and beliefs, and in many ways they will define your brand in their own very personal terms. That's something you must come to appreciate if you are to capture a proposition that is fully alive.

Below are five questions I like to pose to customers, as they can provide a great discussion base for getting at what's truly important.

One word of caution: don't accept vague answers like "You provide good service." While that may be true and good to hear, you can't work with it. Push a bit and ask what good service looks like, how your particular version of good service makes the customer feel, and if they can tell you a story about a specific instance in which they felt they got good service.

## 1. What made you decide to hire us/buy from us in the first place?

This is a good baseline question for your marketing. It can get at how effectively your advertising, message, and lead conversion processes are working. I've also heard customers answer this question by talking about the personal connection or culture that felt right.

## 2. What's one thing we do better than others you do business with?

In this question you are trying to discover something that you can work with as a true differentiator. This is probably the question you'll need to work the hardest at getting specific answers to. You want to look for words and phrases and actual experiences that keep coming up over and over again, no matter how insignificant they may seem to you. If your customers are explaining what they value about what you do, you may want to consider making that the core marketing and positioning message for your business.

### 3. What's one word you would use to describe how you think about our organization?

The one-word-answer question is such an interesting one. If your intended positioning and this word match up, there's a good chance your customers are experiencing your purpose in the ways you intend.

If they do not, one of two things is possible. Either there's a mismatch with how you want to be perceived or you're simply not communicating the things that matter to you most in a way that positions your business in a consistent manner.

### 4. Do you refer us to others? If so, why?

This is the ultimate gauge of customer satisfaction because a truthful answer means your customer likes the product and likes the experience of getting the product.

Small businesses can take this a step further and start examining why they get referrals and perhaps the exact words and phrases a customer might use when describing to a friend why your company is the best.

### 5. What other companies do you love to refer?

Study these companies and try to understand why they do what they do. There's a good chance they can provide clues as to how you can make your "why" a bigger part of your marketing. In addition, you can start building a list of "best of class" companies based on your customers' recommendations. There's a pretty good chance this could be a great list of potential strategic partners.

# The Core Value Propositions

As you develop a marketing strategy for your business, you must
proactively focus on the value proposition of "why us" and build all of
your marketing messages, products, services, processes, and follow-up
communication around supporting that proposition.

This is how you use strategy to dominate your market. This is how
you define value in terms that matter to those you are trying to
attract.

Below are seven ways to think about defining and refining your
core value proposition.

**1. Know your client.** So many companies try to serve mass
audiences. This is tough for any organization, but can be next
to impossible for a small business just getting started. One very
powerful way to create a point of differentiation is to carve out
a narrow segment of a market and explain through every communication that you are the experts in serving that market.

Divorce attorneys who specialize in representing men are an
example of this type of approach. Obviously, you won't attract
female clients, but a man going through a divorce might feel
you have specialized knowledge and experience that other,
more generic divorce attorneys don't possess.

**2. Find a better way.** Creating a product, service, or approach
that clearly offers a better way to get a result, particularly a result
customers desperately need to get, is another strong way to demonstrate value and promote a business.

Everyone struggles with processing too much information.
Many have developed all kinds of systems to remember things,
track things, and keep to-do lists under control. Evernote created a better way to do this and made the process simple, acces-
sible, and manageable on the devices that millions already
used. It offered a very recognizable way to do something better
and the company has grown considerably because of it.

**3. One of a kind.** Some segment of just about every market craves things that are custom made. The more markets are inundated with mass-produced items, the more opportunity exists for things that are made to order or made by hand.

The popularity of a platform like Etsy is due in part to this need to find and possess things that are one of a kind.

If you can find a segment of your market that values this approach, it can be a highly profitable proposition. I asked the owner of a men's clothing shop I frequent about the market for suits these days and he said there are really only two segments left: the low-end off-the-rack suit and the very high-end custom-tailored suit.

**4. Create access.** Another interesting value proposition is to take a market or demand that already exists and disrupt it by creating access that isn't generally available.

Peter Shankman founded a service called HARO or Help a Reporter Out, based on this proposition. PR professionals and marketers had long paid thousands of dollars a year to gain access to a pool of journalists looking for sources to specific stories.

HARO built a database and service based on this concept and made it available to anyone who wished to subscribe for no cost. The service became so popular that it began to attract significant ad revenue and Shankman later sold it to another industry disruptor, Vocus.

**5. Create savings.** Offering ways to save money or lower risk will always be a strong way to differentiate a business. Of course, this is not the same thing as offering a lower price. The key to this proposition is to demonstrate how your product or service will clearly allow the customer to save money through the use of what you are offering. A version of this proposition is to show customers how they can lower the risk of losing money as well.

Cloud-based software services like Dropbox do this very well. Dropbox allows many people to more easily share and store files without the need for server hardware and eliminates the risk of losing data by automatically offering backups.

**6. Be convenient.** Come up with a product, service, or business that makes it more convenient to do something that people are used to doing and you've got the makings of a winning value proposition.

I read a lot of books and the Kindle device for me is flat-out the most convenient way to find, buy, read, store, and carry lots of books around.

**7. Offer great design.** Great design is actually very hard to come by, but when you invest in it as a core value proposition, it can actually be a tremendous way to stand out and attract a market segment for whom form and function are equally important.

Apple has entered and dominated several markets in which they had no history using their design value proposition.

Building a business model and marketing strategy based firmly on any one of these proven propositions will allow you to carve out your place in the market. However, if you can combine several of these propositions, you've got the foundation for something downright disruptive.

An eyewear collaboration between four close friends that eventually became Warby Parker was created as an alternative to what the founders felt was a market full of overpriced and bland eyewear.

According to Neil Blumenthal, cofounder and co-CEO, "We just didn't think a pair of glasses should cost more than an iPhone."

Warby Parker's obvious innovation was to serve the customer directly in an industry full of middlemen, big-name designers, and licensed brand names.

The company designs its line of glasses, works directly with the manufacturers, and sells its line of prescription and sunglasses directly to the end consumer.

In an effort to take on an entrenched $16 billion industry, the company created a fixed price of $95 for all styles, shipped up to five pairs for no-cost test drives prior to purchase, and donated a pair of glasses to those in need for every pair sold.

The company was featured on *CBS Sunday Morning* and in the *New York Times* in 2011, sold over one hundred thousand pairs of glasses, and grew to more than fifty employees according to its 2011 annual report.

Savings, access, convenience, design, and a better way all rolled into one value proposition.

## Turning Stories into an Authentic Proposition

The key to getting the most from the exercise above is to listen intently for the stories your customers tell when you do these interviews. The repetition of themes, either from current customers or those whom you intend to court as customers, is a great place to start as you consider shaping your positioning into an authentic and attractive package.

Now let's blend your findings from your interviews with your higher purpose and run them by a few questions like the following:

- How could we serve our higher purpose doing something that nobody in our industry is doing?
- How could we serve our higher purpose by solving the greatest frustration of our ideal customers?
- How could we serve our higher purpose by creating an obvious innovation in our industry?
- How could we serve our higher purpose by exploring unique ways to package, price, or deliver our products and services?
- How could we serve our higher purpose by creating a totally unique customer experience?

The answers to these kinds of questions may help you start to address the chore of turning purpose to strategy and strategy to message, but mostly this is an attempt to get at what is, or at what should be.

Proper positioning is a story. Not one that you tell, but one that customers tell themselves.

## The Search for Authenticity

The ultimate goal of this chapter is to discover your authentic positioning, not to create one that sounds good.

I find it amusing when businesses strive to be authentic at the direction of the CEO.

Authenticity is simply the manifestation of what you truly believe, the core values, and the basic identity of the leader of the business.

I suppose there are businesses that in the short term can fool people into buying a manufactured brand of authenticity, but in the long run, there's really no hiding what you stand for.

The question is, does what you believe, what you stand for, allow you to build a business that draws people and things that propel the business upward or merely hold it in a constant state of lifelessness?

When you uncover the higher purpose that your business serves, or at least the thing that gives you the most joy, and that becomes the total focus of the business, authenticity simply blooms.

Positioning based in purpose doesn't really care what you sell; it's mostly concerned with why you sell it. This kind of positioning invites others to belong to something that gives them clarity about what they truly believe.

# 7

# Traits of a Fully Alive Business

**The final component of the** fully alive business is personality. This is how you bring purpose to life and make your core message more than words.

If positioning is how you deliver on purpose, then personality is how the world experiences your purpose. Even brilliant positioning is little more than words unless there's a way for people to feel it and connect in the day-to-day flourishes and personality traits that are expressed through the projects and processes they come into contact with.

Businesses that attract may initially do so with a brilliant marketing positioning strategy, but customers experience that strategy and connect and commit to that strategy as they experience tangible personality characteristics, such as the way you follow up or the pleasant surprises you add to their shipments, rather than business features.

Businesses that embrace one or all of the characteristics that are described below as central elements of their decision making, product development, hiring, prioritization, policies, process, and messaging stand a far greater chance of connecting with the people who come into contact with the business because every element is infused with purpose.

These personality traits combine to offer consistent proof of purpose in action and act as a simple guide for action in every department and directive.

The seven personality traits that follow show up time and time again when people are asked for the one word they associate most with companies they love to do business with. Explore this list as you move to complete the strategy part of this book.

Are these traits that people would commonly associate with your business?

The fundamental task of the leader of the fully alive business is to explore ways to infuse every component of the business with these characteristics.

# 1. Inspiration

People want to go on journeys they feel are epic in nature. Now, this may sound a little far-fetched if you're simply building a small law firm focused on small businesses, but every business can inspire.

We can inspire by telling stories, by communicating the why, by standing up for simplicity, and by bravely connecting our own purpose in life with that of the business and that of the goals and objectives of our clients.

Leadership, the kind that's drawn from deed and word, the kind that understands that the best way to get more is to want more for others, is inspirational. Firms that draw commitment from customers and staff give them a way to be their best selves.

Steve Jobs is cited more often than any other company leader for his ability to inspire through telling stories about the Apple brand.

Seth Godin is quite possibly one of the most popular bloggers in the world. His readers are committed to helping him succeed. When Seth mentions a book in a blog post, several hundred people run out and buy it.

I read Seth's books and I enjoy them. But I don't always implement the new strategies and tactics I find in those books. What Seth's books do—in fact what all of Seth's blog posts do—is inspire me. I always come away feeling better for having taken the time to visit, and that, I believe, is one of the secrets to the success of brand Seth.

Despite a ton of competitors, 37signals boasts over 5 million users of online services. The company's customers are fanatical in their support because the software does just what it's supposed to do and little more—that's an inspiring idea. The company inspires through simple ideas and incredible design. People are drawn to the almost counterintuitive innovation that holds on dearly to simplicity. The organization lives these beliefs and has been profitable from day one.

If you or your organization does nothing that inspires, will people commit?

## 2. Innovation

Every industry engages in practices that customers learn to live with. And then someone comes along, either from outside the industry or from the inside, as a means of saving the struggling company, and shakes it up by suggesting there's a better way.

Creating what ends up looking like an obvious innovation in an industry and then embracing that change as a marketing strategy is one way that companies differentiate themselves.

Rackspace, a Web hosting company located in Austin, Texas, created an obvious innovation in the hosting industry by simply making a decision to provide real customer service. While that doesn't seem like an innovation, it happened in an industry that appeared to abhor actually talking to its customers.

To sum up Rackspace's marketing strategy: "Fanatical Support isn't just what we do. It's really what makes us, well, us. It's our need to make a difference in the lives of our customers—no matter how big or small. Really, it's our way of life."

Many years ago, Amazon.com revolutionized the way books were bought and sold by seizing an opportunity and executing in a way that turned them into a dominant, innovative player in the retail industry.

Another Amazon innovation, the Kindle, ushered in mainstream acceptance of the electronic book. E-books are great, but they have one big downside: they're hard to loan. Amazon eventually created the technology that allowed people to loan their Kindle books, but it didn't really facilitate doing so like it did with, say, selling used books.

Lendle.me seized an opportunity for innovation and created an e-book loaning and borrowing service that allows people to rent the e-books they've purchased and borrow from a library created by users.

# 3. Play

People will give their last dollar to be entertained. I believe this has never been more true than it is today. Since so many of the products, services, and ideas we sell can be acquired for free these days, the money is in the package and the experience.

I've had several opportunities to visit the Google campus and they really get this one. Work is often long, hard, and boring, but when do we ever tire of play?

Make your business one that's fun to go to work in, fun to hear from, and fun to do business with, and people will be drawn in.

Step inside the offices of T-shirt maker Threadless and you are greeted by giant stuffed creatures, two Airstream "think pods," offices decorated by staff to show off departmental personality, and a basketball court in the warehouse. The place is definitely fun.

Humor and lightness are powerful tools in the hands of a creative marketer.

Both employees and customers benefit from a business where play and laughter are as treasured as profit and process.

It's not hard to add a little fun and personality to your business. You don't have to become a stand-up comedian, simply look at some of your current communication and follow-up.

Is it boring, dry, and fact-based? Does it sound a little bit like a robot wrote it? Do you send out automated follow-ups that beg to be ignored? How about that out-of-office message? Does it state the default message or does it make someone smile with a delightful little surprise?

Derek Sivers, founder of independent music publisher CD Baby, tells this story about his now-famous package insert.

One day he decided his "thank you for your order" message, inserted in every shipment, was boring and didn't sound like fun at all. So, on a whim, he wrote the note below, and he attributes this bit of silliness with creating more buzz for his organization than anything else he'd ever tried.

Your CDs have been gently taken from our CD Baby shelves with sterilized contamination-free gloves and placed onto a satin pillow.

A team of 50 employees inspected your CDs and polished them to make sure they were in the best possible condition before mailing.

Our packing specialist from Japan lit a candle and a hush fell over the crowd as he put your CDs into the finest gold-lined box that money can buy.

We all had a wonderful celebration afterwards and the whole party marched down the street to the post office where the entire town of Portland waved "Bon Voyage!" to your package, on its way to you, in our private CD Baby jet on this day, Sunday, December 11th.

I hope you had a wonderful time shopping at CD Baby. We sure did. Your picture is on our wall as "Customer of the Year." We're all exhausted but can't wait for you to come back to CDBABY.COM!!

Thank you once again,
Derek Sivers, president,
CD Baby

There are so many ways to add humor, fun, play, and lightness to the workplace and so many good reasons to do it. Consider building a basketball court in the warehouse, letting people decorate the office the way they like, having a formal Friday, sending goofy gifts to customers, answering the phone in odd ways, creating highly personal stories, posting pictures of your staff during craft day, checking your communication and follow-up messages. But most of all, lighten up already.

# 4. Community

The idea of community in business has taken top billing in recent years due in large part to the growth of social networks and the groups of people they foster.

Organizations fortunate enough to have forward-thinking CEOs and marketing departments have even added the role of a community manager.

Thinking about community as anyone that comes into contact with your business will alter the way you view your business.

The popular note-capturing service Evernote actually hired a community member to write what he thought was a better user guide for the service. Evernote paid heed and had this to say after their community member published the guide:

> We're excited to announce the release of Evernote Essentials, the first English-language Evernote handbook (e-handbook, technically). Huzzah!
>
> This excellent Evernote overview was written by blogger, developer and avid tweeter, Brett Kelly. With Evernote Essentials, Brett has created a guide that shows new and experienced users alike the many ways to make the most out of Evernote. Each section comes full of easy to understand explanations, walkthroughs, tips, tricks, and ideas to help anyone become an Evernote ninja.

Brett sent us some early drafts, which impressed us so much that we hired him. Brett is now working on dramatically improving Evernote's own documentation.

# 5. Convenience

Some businesses are hard to do business with. We may love what they do but scratch our heads at how they do it.

Take down the barriers to communication, give people the tools to do what they want, rethink meetings, eliminate the policies of control, trust your customers and staff, and, above all, use technology to enhance personal relationships rather than to wall them off.

Being easy to do business with is a marketing strategy that can become a culture and mantra that spreads word of mouth and drives customer adoption faster than any promotion or campaign ever could.

People will pay more for a convenient experience and you must factor this into every aspect of the business. It's not always the best product that wins. Often it's a good product that is easy to find, easy to understand, and easy to acquire that stays the course.

We often get stuck running our businesses in ways that are most convenient for us and not so much for the very people we need to attract—the customers. Some of the greatest innovations available today reside in making something—a product, service, or entire industry—more convenient.

Start by taking a look at all the ways a prospect could find you and contact you. Are your contact details on every page of your Web site? Do you have outposts in places like Facebook? Are your local search-engine profiles enhanced with useful information? Do you offer multiple forms of contact (e-mail, Web form, click-to-call, IM)? Can prospects get additional information without having to pick up the phone?

# 6. Simplicity

This trait may resemble convenience, but the distinction is great
enough that's it's important to think about them separately.

Life is too complicated and so are instruction manuals, return
policies, messages, mission statements, features, and design.

Simplicity is the most appreciated attribute of the products and
services we love to love. And yet it can be one of the hardest to actually
achieve. It can't be done by simply stripping out features. If this is to
be a marketing strategy, it must become a way of life that informs
every decision.

37signals is a great example of a business that has embraced simplicity as a marketing strategy. They make great software that does
just a handful of things very, very well. According to the CEO, Jason
Fried, they spend more time considering what features to leave out of
a release than what to add in.

The organization lives these beliefs and has been profitable from
day one.

- Useful is forever. Bells and whistles wear off, but usefulness
  never does. We build useful software.
- Our customers are our investors. They fund our daily operations by paying for our products. We answer to them, not to
  outside investors or the stock market.
- Clarity is king. Buzzwords, lingo, and sensationalized
  marketing-speak have no place at 37signals.

# 7. Surprise

Who doesn't like to get unexpected gifts, free overnight shipping,
and handwritten notes? And yet, when was the last time you got any
of those?

Zappos, the online shoe and clothing retailer, has an unstated policy of surprise. If you order shoes on a Monday, the order confirmation will suggest that you allow three to five days for shipping, but don't be surprised if they show up the next morning.

One of my favorite surprise stories involves Bob's Red Mill Natural Foods in Milwaukie, Oregon. The company produces a range of all-natural flours, meals, and grains.

At a company party where employees gathered to help owner Bob Moore celebrate his eighty-first birthday, he surprised the 209 employees by telling them he was giving the company, estimated by some to be worth several hundred million dollars, to the employees by way of an Employee Stock Ownership Program (ESOP). Any employee who had more than three years of service was immediately fully vested. Surprise!

Moore explained it this way in an interview with the *Seattle Times:* "In some ways I had a choice," Moore said of what he could have done with the company he founded with his wife, Charlee, in 1978. "But in my heart, I didn't. These people are far too good at their jobs for me to just sell it."

Those employees who know Moore well were not really that surprised, although the size of the gesture was awe inspiring. To them, he was simply living his purpose and values, the same purpose and values that are evident in the products the company makes, and I'm guessing the same purpose and values that he used to forge commitment with his staff and loyalty with his customer base.

# 8

# The Strategy Workshop

**In this chapter, we are** going to bring everything we've covered so far into your one-page strategy and commitment plan. I'll offer some review and introduce a number of tools you can use to work through the various elements of your plan.

When you complete the strategy workshop, you should have created what amounts to your commitment cheat sheet, a tool I hope you refer to each day as you create or review your to-do list.

The plan should possess the power to inspire you. You may choose not to share this document as it will be written here, but certainly there are elements that will make up the foundation of your internal and external storytelling and teaching.

## The Elements of Strategy

Grab your notebook to record the following:

Passion—**Your Primary Passion Mantra**—this is your personal commitment phrase that sums up your internal drive for life. Go back and review Chapter 2.

_____

_____

_____

Purpose—**Your Higher Purpose Statement**—this is the statement that expresses your company's higher purpose. Go back and review Chapter 4.

_____

_____

_____

Positioning—**Your Core Differentiator**—this is how your purpose is delivered and turns purpose into marketing. Go back and review Chapter 5.

_____

_____

_____

Personality—**Real-Life Characteristics Grid**—these are the ever-present characteristics that determine how your purpose and positioning are experienced. Go back and review Chapter 6.

_____

_____

_____

Choose to infuse your business with one of the following as your core personality trait: simplicity, surprise, play, innovation, value, convenience, community, or inspiration.

Now add others as complementary traits that further deliver how you wish your purpose to be experienced.

_____

_____

_____

## Part 2

# The Patron:
# Culture

# 9

# A Culture of Shared Commitment

**Jake Nickell and Jacob DeHart** started Threadless in 2000 with $1,000. It began as a T-shirt design competition in which Nickell and DeHart invited users to post their designs on a forum thread and promised to print the best designs on T-shirts.

Today, thousands of designers upload their T-shirt designs to the Web site, where visitors and members of the community score them on a scale of zero to five. On average, around 1,500 designs compete in any given week. Each week, the staff selects about ten designs. Each designer selected receives $2,000 in cash, a $500 gift certificate (which they may trade in for $200 in cash), as well as an additional $500 for every reprint.

The current warehouse and office is located in a former printing plant in the West Loop neighborhood of Chicago. The building is open to the public and a handful of customers stop by every day to pick up shirts in person.

The space looks more like what an episode of *Extreme Make-over* might produce for a group of orphaned college students than an office, but somehow the Threadless staff of about forty finds a way to produce and ship over one hundred thousand T-shirts and other goods each month. Threadless doesn't publish revenue numbers, but some quick math would put it in the $30 million range.

When you enter the Threadless offices, you're greeted by large vibrant wall murals, video games, beanbag furniture, go-karts, a giant television, a Ping-Pong table, and several Airstream trailers used as thinking pods and recording studios for videos and podcasts.

Employees take turns as product models for the featured weekly T-shirts and it's not uncommon for a photo shoot to interrupt a game of three-on-three basketball in the warehouse. Each department chooses how their space is decorated and it's safe to say that "eclectic" is the predominant style.

Products selected as winners by the community simply never bomb, as they've been given a life before they are ever produced. The winning designer's story becomes a part of the end product as much as the design itself.

The secret to success at Threadless is the thorough blurring of the lines between company, staff, and customer. It might be easy to conclude that the Threadless founders simply tapped an interesting business model at the right time and then turned it into a business that made a lot of money while they had fun doing it. But that would miss one of the most important elements—the community. The Threadless model depends upon the almost rabid support of its community members, those who submit the designs, vote on the designs, and buy the designs.

It's no surprise that most of the company's employees are drawn from that community. Most come to Threadless wanting to be a part of the staff after developing a passion for the business as a member of the community. Many employees also remain a part of the community and routinely continue to submit and vote on designs as well as engaging other community members.

Many people take warehouse support and janitorial work at Threadless, regardless of their qualifications. Prospective employees are so attracted to the Threadless culture they've already become a part of as a member of the community that they often go to great lengths to join the team.

In this section of the book, we are going to dive deeply into the idea of culture and what it takes to build a workplace that people commit to while building a business that represents something they feel strongly about.

From a practical standpoint, you'll never build any kind of business until you can find people you trust to keep it going when you step away. You'll also never create a fully alive business until you can find, nurture, and build a team of people that you trust so much that you don't have to manage them.

You're passionate and you think about your business day and night, but let's face it, you've got a big vision for that business and you probably can't realize that vision all by yourself.

Your passion and commitment are essential, but it's your ability to build passion and commitment for that vision in others that is going to be the key to growth.

You need committed and connected staff members. You need committed and loyal customers. You need to create a commitment engine that runs without you.

You do this by fostering a business that manufactures ideas, brilliance, passion, and commitment in a community that chooses to join a cause.

Generating commitment is the new currency of American business. The most important task of a leader is to guide passion and purpose in a way that encourages staff and customers alike to find, nurture, and grow commitment around the things big and small that make a business worth joining.

A loyal, committed, paying customer is the ultimate expression of a commitment factory.

Below are a handful of practices to consider in the creation of your self-run commitment engine.

## Get the Right People

Hire for fit is a common bit of advice, but fit means many things. What you need are people who want to excel at the work you need them to do. You need people who ask why you want them to do something instead of just how.

You'll eventually need people who foster purpose, people who invent projects, and people who operate process. These are rarely the same people.

## Tell the Story Over and Over

One of the acts involved in getting the right people is telling a story about why you do what you do in a way that attracts the people you need.

When you connect why with how in the form of a story, you allow people to find their place in the story and that's where commitment starts.

## Protect the Standards

People need to understand how to tell the story in a simple and consistent manner and the symbols, words, and phrases that position the story in the mind of the customer need to be fostered and protected.

Little things like color and typography need to be defined and reinforced. How you speak about your customers sets the tone for how they will be treated by all. How you treat your staff is precisely how they will treat your customers.

These are standards that you need to create, enforce, and leave no room for deviation from.

## Make Meetings About Action

Meetings are where people go to get the life sapped out of them, but it certainly doesn't have to be that way. Most people make meetings about trying to decide what to do when they should be about taking action on what's been decided.

If you run your meetings the latter way, they will be full of life. Then you can install real brainstorming sessions as a way to spark big ideas, refine innovation, and plug gaps in processes.

## Teach and Share the Metrics

In order to get everyone on the same page, they need to be looking at the same page. Your factory needs to know what's important to measure, the key indicators of success, and you need to teach everyone in the business what those key metrics are and what they mean.

This may mean teaching basic accounting measurements to everyone, holding quarterly marketing message training days, and connecting little things, like customer support high fives, to big things like profit.

Creating a system of bonuses tied to key metrics, such as finding ways to reduce costs or convert and retain customers, is how you turn attention on the right things into a game worth playing.

## Invest in the Best Tools

People perform better with the right tools. Combine the best tools with a clear understanding of how to win and you've got a potent combination.

Invest in the best technology you can afford. Invest in chairs, fitness equipment, water, coffee, apps, and music, things some would suggest you could live without, things that help your people stoke their passion and commitment for the work they need to do.

Building a business, even a small, virtual business, is more about building a spirit of commitment around a single-minded purpose than it is about building walls and doors and windows. It's the model for the new factory and it's the future of business that works.

## What Is Culture?

I wish I could give you a crisp definition of what the word *culture* with regard to business really means. It's a tricky word that finds its way into most discussions regarding the workplace these days.

Like so many things, it's hard to describe, but just as I knew when I first visited the Threadless offices in Chicago, you know it when you see it.

Every business has a culture; it may be strong or weak, positive or negative, or just plain hard to spot, but it's like an internal brand in a way. It's the collective impression, habits, language, style, communication, and practices of the organization.

Some elements of culture are intentional; some are accidental. Some are rooted deeply in the ethos of the original employee group, and some are created out of a lack of any real direction or clarity.

My belief is that a healthy culture is a shared culture, one created through shared stories, beliefs, purpose, plans, language, outcomes, and ownership.

These aren't little things; these aren't things you get right during an annual retreat. These are things molded over time with trust and passion and caring. These are things that evolve.

I don't have all the answers, but I can assure you that this is the question that needs answering: how can I build a culture of shared commitment?

# The Elements of Shared Commitment

The following elements make up the foundation of a system of
shared commitment. I list them here as an overview and introduction and will go into each more deeply in the remaining chapters of
this section.

## Shared Stories

The first step is to begin to develop, archive, curate, and tell stories
about the business that illustrate what the business stands for.

Stories that tell why you do what you do, whom you do it for, why
you're passionate about it, and where the business is headed.

Throughout time, great leaders have used stories to inspire commitment and attract community.

The central elements of a strong culture are the stories that
employees tell themselves and one another. You'll need to have a
story for each situation that your employees might face. These illustrations are like oral traditions that allow culture to sustain, thrive,
and grow, and it's the job of the leader of the business to make story
building an intentional act.

## Shared Beliefs

As I've stated previously, people want to work for more than a paycheck. Sure, they want to be paid fairly and in some cases the element
of salary will be an important aspect of their decision to come to work
for an organization, but perhaps more important, people want to
work on something they believe in and they want to do that work with
people who share their passion and beliefs.

This isn't the same as saying everyone in your organization has to
maintain the same beliefs. However, by creating a set of core beliefs
that everyone in the organization lives by and supports, you create
a set of standards for how decisions are made, how people treat one

another, how they treat customers, what's expected, how to manage, and even how to write a sales letter.

## Shared Purpose

In order to bring purpose fully into the organization, you must determine a way to bring it to life and reinforce it in every decision the organization makes.

This may take the form of an employee development program, foundation support, benefit package, or "Dream Manager" program. The key is to bring purpose to life through example. Your actions, or how you treat your staff, will speak far louder about purpose than any page in an employee manual. In order to create a shared purpose, the staff must be your first customer.

## Shared Plans

The strongest, most productive cultures come to life when people know what to do and how to do it. These are places where people are trusted to do good work and use their creativity to solve problems.

If you are to grow your organization to the point where it can serve your ultimate higher purpose, you'll need to develop a system that enables people to manage themselves.

Now, that may sound a little foreign or perhaps even scary to anyone who's worked in a typical hierarchical business structure, but it's central to a fully alive culture.

The key lies in systematic planning, thinking, clear accountability, and consistent communication.

## Shared Leadership

While stories are an important way to attract and inspire people to join you on your journey, they can only take you as far as the leaders you develop around you.

After payroll is made and a business is generating sufficient cash flow, I really believe that the leader's primary role should shift to developing leaders internally.

In fact, as the owner of a business, you'll never succeed in reaching beyond where you are today until you are no longer the person who brings in the most work.

Teaching others to land the big fish, to tell stories, to create shared beliefs, to inspire and attract commitment means you have to invest time and resources in this very thing in a very intentional way.

This element of the shared culture comes by teaching your people what an ideal customer looks like, what a customer is desperately in need of, and how to communicate your core point of differentiation in a meaningful way. It comes by teaching what everything costs, how profit is made, and how every decision impacts a customer in some way. It grows by sending employees to school, supporting their growth in other areas, and demonstrating that yours is an organization that cares for the whole person.

## Shared Outcomes

One of the strongest ways to foster commitment is to get people to commit to a stake in the outcome of their work.

The only way I know to do this is to establish benchmarks, goals, and indicators and then report and communicate progress religiously.

You must create reporting mechanisms that truly measure the most important components of your business. This will include key financial elements but must strive to go far beyond into measuring success around shared beliefs and culture.

## Shared Ownership

The ultimate measure of commitment is achieved when people who work for your organization come to understand that they play a crucial role in creating the kind of company they want to work for—that the company is actually their most important product. (Of course, the owner has to realize that first.)

This won't happen until you help your people free themselves from the typical job descriptions and organization charts so they can begin to manage themselves. It won't happen unless they are excited about the journey they are on. It won't happen until they fully understand how a dollar spent on a new desk equates to profit margin.

It won't happen until they start thinking like an owner when it comes to meeting a customer's needs. It won't happen until everyone realizes they can help develop new business, build the community, create innovation, fix problems, right wrongs, and make decisions that impact the organization on their own.

# 10

# Sharing Something Heroic

**People ache to go on** journeys that are meaningful, epic, and seem heroic. That doesn't mean everyone wants to be a hero, but I do think we want to be a part of something that feels like it's worth doing.

And that feeling, that connection, often comes from a shared story. A simple story can draw upon our emotional desires in ways that reams and reams of logical data never will.

Consider this story told in an annual e-mail blast by Scott Heiferman, cofounder and CEO of Meetup, about the event that moved him to start a business some thought was crazy.

> I don't write to our whole community often, but this week is special because it's the 10th anniversary of 9/11 and many people don't know that Meetup is a 9/11 baby.
>
> Let me tell you the Meetup story. I was living a couple miles from the Twin Towers, and I was the kind of person who thought local community doesn't matter much if we've got the Internet and TV. The only time I thought about my neighbors was when I hoped they wouldn't bother me.

When the towers fell, I found myself talking to more neighbors in the days after 9/11 than ever before. People said hello to neighbors (next-door and across the city) who they'd normally ignore. People were looking after each other, helping each other, and meeting up with each other. You know, being neighborly.

A lot of people were thinking that maybe 9/11 could bring people together in a lasting way. So the idea for Meetup was born: Could we use the Internet to get off the Internet—and grow local communities?

We didn't know if it would work. Most people thought it was a crazy idea—especially because terrorism is designed to make people distrust one another. A small team came together, and we launched Meetup 9 months after 9/11.

Today, almost 10 years and 10 million Meetuppers later, it's working. Every day, thousands of Meetups happen. Moms Meetups, Small Business Meetups, Fitness Meetups . . . a wild variety of 100,000 Meetup Groups with not much in common—except one thing.

Every Meetup starts with people simply saying hello to neighbors. And what often happens next is still amazing to me. They grow businesses and bands together, they teach and motivate each other, they babysit each other's kids and find other ways to work together. They have fun and find solace together. They make friends and form powerful community. It's powerful stuff. It's a wonderful revolution in local community, and it's thanks to everyone who shows up.

Meetups aren't about 9/11, but they may not be happening if it weren't for 9/11. 9/11 didn't make us too scared to go outside or talk to strangers. 9/11 didn't rip us apart. No, we're building new community together! The towers fell, but we rise up. And we're just getting started with these Meetups.

## Great Leaders Are Great Storytellers

Today's most successful companies are led by people who create, nurture, curate, and tell the organization's most important stories. The leader creates the story, lives the story, keeps the story alive, and coaches everyone in the organization to tell the story.

Useful company stories are like artifacts; they are chosen, passed around, and kept alive by compiling many of the right parts and using them in the perfect context.

It's said that Southwest Airlines founder Herb Kelleher was a legendary storyteller. Quite possibly his most famous story detailed an ongoing battle with a competitor airline in the early days of the company. The story is chronicled in great detail in Kevin and Jackie Freiberg's book *Nuts!**

The story, dubbed "Malice in Dallas," documents a friendly contest between Southwest Airlines, represented by Herb Kelleher, and Stevens Aviation, championed by chairman Kurt Herwald, to decide the rights to a slogan. Stevens, an aviation sales and maintenance company in Greensville, South Carolina, had been using "Plane Smart" as its slogan at least one year before Southwest unknowingly began infringing with its "Just Plane Smart" ad campaign.

After bringing this to Southwest's attention, Stevens Aviation proposed that, rather than paying teams of lawyers to hash out the dispute over many months and under cover of hundreds of thousands of dollars in fees, the companies send their top warriors to battle it out, one-on-one, in an arm-wrestling tournament before an audience of their employees and the media.

According to the Freibergs, "Malice in Dallas" is now an epic story that thousands of people inside and outside Southwest Airlines know almost by heart. This rambunctious alternative to a drawn-out, boring, half-million-dollar courtroom battle was exactly the

---

* Kevin and Jackie Freiberg, *Nuts! Southwest Airlines' Crazy Recipe for Business and Personal Success* (New York: Crown Business, 1998), 246–49.

sort of antics that Americans have come to associate with their favorite maverick airline.

Many businesses have grasped some level of success based on the founder's ability to tell a visionary story about the business, product, service, or results before they are a reality. I wonder how much business has been won on the heartfelt belief that "if they buy it, we'll figure out how to make it."

Great leaders are natural storytellers, but even business owners who would never readily consider themselves to be great leaders often can't help but tell their story so passionately that those who listen simply want to believe.

## Four Stories Every Business Must Build

The real power of storytelling is that it permits a business to illustrate values and beliefs in action.

It's one thing to say you're trustworthy and quite another to share a story about the day your employees went without a paycheck because they so believed in what you were building and trusted you would make things right.

I believe that all businesses must find and tell core stories over and over again and then they must invite their employees, customers, and networks to help build these stories into journeys worth taking over and over again.

Below are four core stories that must live in every business.

### The Passion Story

This is often the owner's story, a tale of why they started the business and how the business serves their own personal mission or purpose in life. Why they get up and go to work, why they love what they do, or what happened in life that set them on their current path.

Leah Beck, a life coach and founder of LaunchPoint Coaching, told me her passion in these words:

Choosing what I wanted to be when I grew up wasn't really an option. Born into poverty and abuse, my focus was on survival. Despite having some incredible hurdles, I lifted myself out of harsh circumstances through hard work, a passion for excellence and stubborn determination. I made it my mission to leverage the lessons that adversity gave me.

I started my career at the bottom. Determined to give my best, promotions came steadily and I moved into management quickly. Using those hard-earned life skills, I discovered I had a natural talent for building businesses.

Details never bothered me. Huge projects and lofty visions thrilled me. I never questioned my ability to tackle the challenges, rally the troops, and harness talent. I never questioned success. I knew intuitively that the road to success was about taking action every single day as though the desired outcome was already present. I was my "launch-point" and my success began and ended with me.

Like many of you, my work took me through a series of business acquisitions and mergers. When I wasn't focused on implementing, I was focused on integrating services, only to later coordinate efforts to pull them apart. These experiences wore at me. I felt restless and tired of being immersed in a career that didn't reflect my highest aspirations. I was making a good living, but something was amiss.

In 2007, I realized that the time had come for me to choose what I wanted to be "when I grew up." My life experience had taught me two primary lessons; first, that no matter what circumstances you are born into, the outcome of your life is based on what you make of it, and second, life is meant to be lived on purpose. When I contemplated the purpose of my life, I knew that I wanted to give others what I had needed most to succeed—support, structure, and accountability with specific actionable work plans.

## The Purpose Story

This is the story about why you do what you do in business. For many people it can be a story about a mission or higher calling, but it can also be about who you serve and why.

When I was just starting to dream up the concept of Duct Tape Marketing, I was operating my business as a traditional local marketing agency and doing work for organizations large and small, although I had already determined that I loved working with small-business owners the most.

I had completed a very small amount of work for a very large organization and sent them an invoice for $1,525. When they paid the invoice, ninety days later, I opened the envelope and found a check for $152,500.

While there was a moment of temptation, I knew I had to return the check. I called and was directed to the five forms I needed to complete in order to return the check if I was to have any hope of getting my original bill paid.

The experience was a turning point for me personally and professionally, as it was the day that I determined I had to take my passion for growing small businesses and make it the higher purpose that my business served. It was the day I determined that I would never again work with people I did not respect. It was the day I determined concretely that the higher purpose my business was meant to serve was to help small-business owners find their purpose and joy through the successful growth of their businesses.

That was the day I fired all but my small-business clients and set out to create a brand that would become a trust beacon for small business. That seemingly innocuous event, played out on an otherwise unmemorable Tuesday afternoon, was my calling to spend the rest of my life opening small-business owners to the unlimited possibilities available through the creation of a fully alive business.

And that's part of my purpose story.

## The Value Proposition Story

This is the story that illustrates how you want the market to perceive your brand. Of course, perception is partly a goal and partly a mea-

surement because some things are out of your hands. A true value proposition story, however, is one that authentically captures your purpose in action. It's how purpose is packaged in a way that allows the intended market to connect to your business.

The best stories can usually be summed up in one word.

Early on in my marketing consulting business, I was invited to be part of a pitch for a very large piece of business. It was a national firm that wanted to hire a national ad agency but also include a local marketing support company for the local branch.

The New York ad agency sent five people, all clad in black head to toe and armed with a hundred-page presentation deck filled with research and recommendations.

When it came time for me to offer my two cents, I said something like "I don't know, why don't we just talk to some of your current customers?" The meeting ended and the next day the VP who was conducting the search called and said he wanted me to do the entire project without the New York ad agency. To this day I can hear him say why: "You were the only one that said anything that was practical."

For my ideal clients, the harried small-business owners trying to do more each day, the idea that what I have to offer is actionable, unpretentious, and above all practical is the true value proposition that my brand stands for and it runs through every decision we make as an organization, every recommendation we attach our name to, and every element of our message, right down to the furniture in our office.

And that's part of my positioning story.

## The Personality Story

This is the story that gets at how people experience your purpose or brand. This is the story that illustrates the traits that are on display in every action, product, service, decision, hire, process, or promotion.

There's a story behind how I came up with the name Duct Tape Marketing, but the real reason this name has served my brand so well has to do with the association people have between duct tape and practicality. This allows them to connect their own personal stories of simple, effective, and affordable use to this gray sticky stuff.

The name comes packaged with its own positive personality traits and the only trick is to make sure that people experience the brand and the business that same way.

And now for where the name came from . . . with apologies to my daughters.

My wife and I decided to take a little minivacation and figured the two oldest girls (high school sophomore and junior) could act as babysitters. You probably know where this is going and you're right.

The party peaked at about one hundred people, I'm told. One of the guests decided to take my car for a spin and bumped it into something just hard enough to knock off a piece of plastic bumper. In an effort to hide the damage, my daughters masterfully duct-taped the piece back in place.

There is a chance they would have gotten away with it too, but they carelessly left the roll of duct tape sitting on the car hood, creating immediate suspicion when we arrived home.

The thing is, that's when I knew Duct Tape Marketing would be the perfect name. If a sixteen-year-old could recognize the simplicity, effectiveness, and affordability of the product, then it might just be universally true as well.

These three little words, *duct tape marketing*, pack a great personality punch and allow people to immediately connect with who we are, what we stand for, and what they can expect from us. It's a lot like meeting someone for the first time and having an impression about the things they believe in before you ever discuss anything with them.

The personality story helps to capture characteristics that positively identify your higher purpose.

And that's part of my personality story.

Here are some resources to help you create and tell your business story:

- *The Story Factor* by Annette Simmons
- *The Leader's Guide to Storytelling* by Stephen Denning
- National Storytelling Network, www.storynet.org
- Center for Digital Storytelling, www.storycenter.org

## The Extraordinary Craft of Story Building

I believe the best leaders are great storytellers, but I also believe the reality of a purpose-filled business asks leaders to become great story builders.

It's not enough to know your story. In order to truly generate commitment, you must help your employees, customers, and networks build their passion and purpose stories into journeys worth taking over and over again.

- We must include our vision for the future, but that vision should be a shared vision.
- We must know everything we can about the goals, hopes, and dreams of a very narrowly defined ideal client (i.e., I am a small-business owner trying to take my business to the next level; I target small-business owners trying to take their business to the next level).
- We must frame our story with a message that addresses the desires, challenges, and unmet needs of this market.
- We must involve customers in the finishing of the story by making their real-life experiences central to the character development and part of the plot.

If you want to take this next giant step in evolving your marketing in a way that turns your customers and prospects into collaborative partners and story builders, sit down with a handful of your ideal customers and ask them the following questions with an eye on developing an extraordinary marketing story.

- What do you know about where this business is going that no one else knows?
- What is your industry's greatest flaw?
- If your business could choose a new identity, what would it be?
- What is your favorite customer story?
- What is your secret wish for your business?
- What is the greatest challenge your business must overcome?
- What is your greatest fear for your business?
- What is your greatest achievement/disappointment?
- What about your childhood shaped you for this moment?
- What choices have you made that you regret?

It may take some guts to pose questions like this to your best customers, but do it and you'll be on your way to building a relationship that can't be penetrated by a competitor's low-cost offers.

# 11

# Committed Beliefs

**One of the tactics used** by many companies to help simplify what the company stands for in a way that generates commitment is through a list of stated core values or what I call "commitment beliefs."

Now, it's quite possible you've worked for an organization that's hung a list of impressive-sounding attributes on a wall somewhere that said "here's what we stand for." Maybe you've done this in your business.

Of course, for this to be anything more than an exercise, you have to live your beliefs. That's why the stories are so important; they become tangible illustrations of what's real.

Every company has a set of core beliefs, some positive, some negative. They're a lot like your brand; you can't really hide it or fake it because ultimately it comes through in who you're being, how the leadership team treats employees and customers, and how you respond to adversity.

The key to leveraging your core beliefs is to find a way to capture the best of what your organization stands for and create, instill, and live those things as often as you can.

To start the process, we return to a few of those powerful questions we posed in the first section of this book. What don't you want in your life? What do you want in your life? Whom do you want to be a hero for? What are your superpowers?

It's the notes from these sessions that will provide some clues for how to translate some of your personal beliefs into the language of commitment for the entire organization.

This process can be a little frustrating and highly personal, but what about generating purpose isn't?

## Create

The key to creating a great list of commitment beliefs is to throw off any notion of what they should be and simply brainstorm a bit about the best traits of your organization. Think about your people. Who on your team embodies what your company stands for?

Gather your leadership team and spend some time truly brainstorming attributes that feel right, that inspire, that you've seen and heard used by staff and customers, and record as many as you like. I know this will sound a little corny to some, but you're looking for words and phrases that have the power to send a chill through the room.

You might even consider including a handful of customers in this exercise. Ask them to describe what they experience as a customer. You might be surprised how insightful some of their comments are.

Once you have a list that seems comprehensive, it's time to start paring it down to the most essential elements that are true beliefs. There is no perfect number, but as you move to make these beliefs the foundation of your message and story, there's a case to be made for less is more. Strive for six or seven candidates for the final list.

Once more for emphasis: This is not a list of what ought to be or what sounds impressive. This is a list of what is, even if what is today isn't as fully developed as you know it can be.

For example, here's a list for my organization:

1. Practice your magic—do what you preach.
2. Simplify everything—elegance over complexity.

**3.** Extend trust—give what you need to earn.
**4.** Make progress—failure is okay.
**5.** Everyone leads—teach and learn.
**6.** Create more—the value equation.
**7.** Be a gift—love each other.

The idea behind these seven elements is that we try to live them in our interactions with one another, our customers, and the market as a whole. They become what we communicate as elements of our brand, but more important we use them to make decisions both individually and as an organization.

## Instill

Radio Flyer, manufacturer of iconic red wagons and tricycles, publicly rewards its employees for abiding by the company's values.

*VALUES:*
We follow the "Little Red Rule": Every time we touch people's lives, they will feel great about Radio Flyer because of our passionate commitment to the FLYER code:

- **FU**Nominal Customer Experiences
- **L**ive with Integrity
- **Y**es I Can
- **E**xcellence in Everything
- **R**esponsible for Sustainability

## Live

All the brainstorming sessions, meetings, and bronze plaques in the world won't bring any life to your stated core values unless you live them and reinforce them in your everyday acts and decisions.

Your commitment beliefs must become part of the story that employees share with new hires.

Committing to this practice can prove to be expensive in the short run but will pay off in the long run.

John Ratliff from Appletree Answers recounts a story about an employee who was found to be effectively stealing by manipulating lead sources and falsifying reports. Appletree immediately let him go, but was faced with a decision after a large sale that the employee had worked on came through, creating a commission of several thousand dollars.

"We knew that no one in the organization would have faulted us for keeping that commission, but that was not the point. The money was due him and in accord with our 'Integrity Matters' belief, we determined paying him was the right thing to do."

Ratliff claims that writing that check was hard at the time, but doing so did more to bring life to the value of integrity than any amount of words could do.

Commitment beliefs have to be reinforced at every turn. Share them in your internal communications, organize monthly themes around them, make them part of the hiring process, and create rewards and recognition around them.

Select strategic objectives and goals in areas related to your core beliefs. Use them to frame decisions, as part of employee reviews, and to solve customer challenges.

When you draw from a small set of positive beliefs and consistently return to them as a way of doing business, you develop a language that starts to become the mind-set for every employee and ultimately dictates how your customers and the public experience your brand.

# 12

# Staff as Customer

**If you ever discover that** your business has a customer service problem, or an accounts receivable problem, or a lead conversion problem, you may end up discovering that what you really have is a people problem.

Your staff is probably treating your customers about the same way you are treating your staff. As I've said in many ways in this book, a healthy customer community is often the natural result of a healthy internal culture. While most organizations focus only on serving the customers, a commitment-filled business views the staff as the primary customer.

## Hire for Fit

When we get to a thorough discussion on community building in part three of this work, I'll argue that the best customer is one who's a good fit for your business. The same holds true for employees. The best employee is one who's a good fit for the work that you do.

The best way to hire for fit is to attract for fit. By putting your business purpose, beliefs, practices, and actions on display as the leading element of your brand, you stand the best chance of attracting prospective employees who want to be a part of your internal community.

There's nothing wrong with being very specific about what kind of commitment you're looking for and what you're not looking for.

Here are some words about fit from the Sky Factory, a business that manufactures unique ceiling and wall installations that use video and images to create an illusion of natural surroundings like clouds and trees:

"Slackers don't last long at the Sky Factory, nor [do] people who aren't comfortable with accountability, flexibility, self-improvement, teamwork, and a little whittling away of the ego."

The Sky Factory, even with a clear sense of hiring for fit, was experiencing a higher level of turnover than they wanted. When they met as a team to try to tackle the issue, they went over a list of all the people who had left or had been fired and tried to come up with some common reasons.

What they discovered was something that most organizations know but find hard to put into words. There were no surprises really on the list of people who had been fired; "all of them just didn't quite feel right."

Often in the hiring process we focus on the logical—the résumé, the words, the answers—and not enough on intuition, but often our intuition can tell us things that our logical brain won't.

The Sky Factory has an interview process that involves fact and skill tests, but then expands the interview process to include as many as twelve individual in-person interviews. The group of twelve will be asked to give a green, yellow, or red impression ranking based on how they felt about the prospect's fit.

This isn't a perfect system, but since installing this process, the company hasn't made one hire who wasn't a good fit.

# Staff as Lead Generator

Even in a down economy, or perhaps particularly in a down economy, engaging your staff in the recruiting process is one of the most
effective ways to build your team.

Organizations that get this find that it is not only easier to fill
positions but that their cost per hire goes down, they increase the
chance that candidates are a good culture fit, and eventual hires
come into the organization with a potential built-in support network.

Creating an environment where current staff members willingly
participate in recruitment takes more than a mention at the quarterly
all-hands meeting. It must become something that is communicated
and amplified at every turn.

The following elements should be considered when creating a
team recruitment program.

## Develop Program Rules

You must make team recruitment an important initiative and that
requires creating a formal program that gets baked into all employee
training and included in the employee handbook.

You need to create rules, or at least spell out how to win, if you
want people to play.

## Create a Budget

Put some money into this program so that people know you are serious. With placement fees from outside firms running in the tens of
thousands, you can easily make a case for $1,000 to $4,000 rewards
for those who bring in a great hire.

Help people understand that this can become a part of their
compensation for helping the organization meet its objectives.

## Post Job Descriptions

Make sure you communicate your hiring needs frequently and in such a way that every employee has the opportunity to participate fully in a referral process.

The mere fact that you communicate your growth needs can have a positive impact on morale as a whole.

## Base Reward on Position Filled

Create a sliding-scale reward program so that everyone can participate and everyone is motivated across the board.

If you need a junior assistant and a VP of finance, create the kind of internal reward that would get employees to tap their networks.

You might also consider mixing up reward programs and offering quarterly travel winners, nonprofit partners, and raffles to keep people interested and motivated.

## Skill-Based Referral

In some instances you might need to incentivize employees just to get you in front of leads who possess very specific skills.

If you're a software company that needs Ruby programmers for a hot market, you may need to consider rewards that get you in the game, even if those leads don't get hired.

## Support Social Media

Many organizations cringe at the prospect of employees participating in social media on behalf of the organization, but enabling social networks is one of the fastest ways for your employees to share your hiring needs with their connections.

Some social networks have even created recruiting platforms that make it easier for organizations to tap their staff's social networks. LinkedIn's Referral Engine program is one such program.

Getting your employees involved in building your team allows them to impact their workplace and helps build a deeper sense of ownership in the direction of the organization.

## Traits in Your Next Hire

Most people interpret *fit* to imply "fit only with the culture of the organization." While I agree, of course, that your recruitment should aim to attract people who share your mission, vision, and values, it's also essential to consider how they might fit in the new reality of business.

There is a specific skill set required these days in order to be successful in the world of business and you need to start finding ways to uncover these skills in the people you recruit.

Most of these skills aren't taught directly and come more naturally to some than others, but an employee who lacks them, or worse, questions them, is going to contribute significantly less to your organization.

While I can define the new skills, you still have to find the ways to unearth them and bring them out in your culture and your employees.

The good news is that these are the same qualities it takes for any business to compete, and if you can make these qualities the central theme of your hiring, they will carry over into the central theme of your business in general.

**Collaboration bias.** Today's business teams are as fluid as ever. They move from project to project, plug and play with virtual members, and draw from around the globe. Work today is basically collaboration on all fronts. If any past experience matters, it's experience that demonstrates ease with contribution and collaboration. Some people thrive on this way of work; some people don't.

**Design character.** Creative people just see the world a little differently than most, and when this ability is balanced with stated business objectives, it can be a powerful tool. Look for people who demonstrate a feel for design, even though that may not be their primary or even secondary function. Creativity in design easily blends over into creativity in ideas, problem solving, and collaboration.

**Social knack.** Recent college grads take note: social business is not Facebook. Social knack isn't a tech platform at all. It is a skill that engages your ability to have a great conversation, to know how to find what makes people tick, to present ideas to a group, and to automatically look for ways to help others get what they want. If your staff inherently possesses these qualities, they can make whatever the tool of the week is pay.

**Tech-curious.** Technology is an incredible playing-field-leveling tool in the hands of smart business owners. Blending high-tech capabilities with high-touch customer experience is the killer play in today's plugged-in world. Employees who are curious about new technology and gadgets as a means to create a better, deeper, and richer customer experience are a must. Hire self-proclaimed nerds and let them fuse the technology with proven processes.

**Bundle vision.** This is quite likely the hardest quality to identify (certainly in a thirty-minute interview) but it may be one of the most important. Business, technology, tools, and trends evolve so quickly these days that every business owner and every staff member needs the ability to appreciate how seemingly disparate parts might come together to make something remarkable. This is perhaps a combination of all of the traits described above, and when you find this trait and hone it, it will become one of the most valuable assets of your business.

## Beliefs in Action

The Kansas City–based digital marketing agency VML was founded out of a desire to create a company that was different from the traditional firms in which the founding partners of VML had spent their careers.

Their goal was to build a company that did work that compelled people to act with purpose. But first and foremost they wanted to create a company where community, including the welfare of the staff as well as the communities where the staff lived, would thrive and grow.

To that end, they made certain that pro bono work took a high priority, that civic and community participation was a core belief, and that they would support the organizations and missions that their staff cared about first.

Community, both internal and external, is front and center in each weekly meeting and the weekly internal newsletter. Once a month, one employee's community participation is recognized by her peers with the award of a $500 gift card.

Every new hire is told about the VML Foundation as part of the interview process and every response to an RFP includes a thorough description of the VML Foundation and community efforts.

VML's "beliefs in action" often spill over into their client community. VML client Kellogg's teamed up with the nonprofit Action for Healthy Kids with the goal of donating a million breakfasts to underserved kids during the 2011–12 school year.

VML used the occasion of National Breakfast Day to voluntarily throw their support into the effort and sponsored a company-wide "share your breakfast" event that raised awareness and breakfasts for the Action for Healthy Kids initiative.

# Higher Purpose

Once Mary and Tom Miller, founders of Jancoa, discovered that the higher purpose of their business was to change the quality of life of their employees by changing their view of the future, they knew they had to invest in a way to make this higher purpose come to life every day in their business. Thus they created the Dream Manager, a program that grew from an employee retention program into an inspiring example of what a business can be.

Through one-on-one coaching sessions and group classes, employees are encouraged to identify their dreams and take real steps to achieve those dreams.

Some dreams that were conceived and accomplished by program participants have included:

- Furthering their education by earning a GED and college degree
- Purchasing a home or automobile
- Starting a small business
- Stopping smoking
- Creating their own Dream Manager charities
- Adopting a child
- Launching individual and team fitness and wellness programs

The spirit of the program has impacted the entire staff in one way or another. One employee stated that his dream was to learn to play a musical instrument but that class times conflicted with his work schedule. Another employee jumped in and traded shifts for the time period so that the aspiring musician could attend the classes and pursue his dream.

"We're disguised as janitors," Mary says, "but it's really about helping people be their best, to be who they really are. I'm just so proud of the people we have and appreciative of them doing such a great job."*

## Continuous Learning

Radio Flyer created Wagon U in an effort to install a formal platform of staff development.

In the words of Chief Wagon Officer Robert Pasin, "If there's one thing I can say about Radio Flyer's proud heritage, it's that we have always kept learning and changing. We would not be where we are today if it weren't for our desire for discovering 'what's next'

---

* Matthew Kelly, *The Dream Manager* (New York: Hyperion, 2007).

and our willingness to try new things, learn from our mistakes, and keep helping each other become better at everything we do.

"By establishing Wagon U, we made a clear statement that we are committing to being a learning organization and providing a platform to take our team to a new level of performance. We are strengthening what's good and helping to make more about us great."

Wagon U includes on-site classes, self-study resources, recommended off-site classes, and an "Ask the Expert Network."

## Volunteer in the Community

VML employees voluntarily participate (73 percent in 2011) in the company's foundation, choosing to make a financial donation with each paycheck. The funds are then awarded as grants to organizations that apply or that are nominated by staff members.

Each year the company sponsors VML Foundation Day, when all seven hundred U.S. employees go out and lend a hand with a number of nonprofit agencies. Every employee also receives two paid volunteer days when they may choose to provide service to the organization of their choice.

## Support the Whole Person

Companies that generate total commitment go beyond simply providing competitive benefits. They view their job as supporting the entire person.

Of course, this comes out loud and clear in an effective set of core beliefs, but it also rings true in the kinds of things you demonstrate by taking action.

In addition to a very strong health care package, the benefits at 37signals include $100 a month toward a gym membership, $100 a month to be used for Community Supported Agriculture (CSA: a popular way for consumers to buy local, seasonal food directly from

a farmer), and an all-expenses-paid vacation to one of several desti-
nations.

The Sky Factory also gives some clues about how they support the
whole person by way of this statement: "We spend most of our time
designing and making products for our clients, but lately we've been
planting an organic chestnut tree orchard, starting bee hives, and
figuring out the best alternative energy source for the factory."

# 13

## Commitment Planning

**Every business that grows and** thrives internally and externally figures out how to manage three things at all times: purpose, projects, and process.

Formed in 2002, the Sky Factory is a company of thirty-five people in a twelve-thousand-square-foot facility on five acres in Fairfield, Iowa. The company produces photo-realistic illusions of nature and installs the backlit images in ceilings and walls.

One of the Sky Factory's core cultural principles is something they call "flat-hive management." The Sky Factory does not have a hierarchical system of management; there are no managers or supervisors. Instead, it's a "bottom-up" organization of self-motivated individuals who participate in multiple job teams and take periodic responsibility as the "facilitator" for one or more groups. The goal (recognized as unachievable, though worthwhile) is that everyone should know and be able to do everything. Individuals rotating through different jobs and teams as well as transparency support this goal.

Committed planning and the recognition of the need for self-management is how you build a culture of commitment like that embodied by the Sky Factory.

Lots of employees come into businesses hoping to rise to the ranks of management. While every employee in a business is ideally a manager of something, lots of business owners start a business and quickly realize the opposite, that they themselves must manage everything.

As a customer, if you enjoy a remarkable experience with a business, there's a very good chance that the experience was given the complete attention of management, but what really made it remarkable was that it didn't feel managed at all.

No matter how simple or complex a business may seem, it must do the following if it is to come to life: communicate purpose as strategy, deliver innovation, growth, and positioning through the implementation of project after project, and create a remarkable culture and consistent customer experience through the operation of process after process.

No matter how many people actually go to work in a business, every business needs to fill the roles of purpose manager, project manager, and process manager even if all three of these roles are played by the same person.

The role of the purpose manager is to create and tell the story of why the business does what it does, create and keep the picture of where the business is headed, and act as the gatekeeper for business decisions made in the name of the brand's positioning.

The role of the project manager is to continually look to break down every business innovation, question, challenge, initiative, or campaign into logical projects complete with required action steps and resources.

The role of the process manager is to receive and implement the tasks and actions for each project plan and implement established processes that ensure consistency.

No matter how complicated we want to make our businesses, success comes down to basic planning.

This is what makes owning a business such a challenge, this is what makes managing people such a challenge, and this is what makes doing a job such a challenge. Finding the places where these three roles divide and where they come back together again is the art of the business, and it's not always obvious and rarely does it come naturally.

If you're the sole employee, you must spend some part of each day playing these distinct roles no matter if your innate talents may reside squarely in only one.

As you hire staff, you must focus first on hiring for your weaknesses in performing or managing one or more of the three roles.

As you grow your business, you must build purpose, project, and process thinking into every new department, innovation, and initiative.

You must also guide your entire team to approach their work in this manner and give them the tools that will allow them to embrace purpose, think in terms of projects, and know when and how process delivers purpose.

## The Committed Plan

*Planning* is a word that draws many different reactions. Some reactions fall to the side of indifference, while others reside firmly in the camp of disdain.

In this chapter, we are going to uncover a planning process that allows you to start bringing to life everything that we've worked on to this point for the entire staff. You'll also find that through this process you can begin to gain the insights and skills needed to build your business block by block as you grow.

Note that I'm not asking you to make a business plan or create a marketing plan—plans aren't the secret; planning is. It's the continuous process of planning, acting, and measuring that moves the organization in the direction of its goals, not the plan document you might create.

Using and teaching the process contained in this chapter is one of the ways you can empower your staff to know they are taking right action on the most important things at all times and knowing this brings a confidence that is a commitment generator in itself.

Commitment planning is a management style that frees your people to be creative instead of forcing them to be bound by a process-only, system-driven activity.

Planning is not a one-day event or even a year-end activity. Sure, there may be certain time-bound planning periods that occur naturally, say at the end of a quarter, but the real way to keep commitment alive is to live it through a creative process that allows everyone to focus on the things that matter most.

To me, the greatest benefit of any planning session is that it helps you decide what not to do.

There's always more to do than you can possibly get done and what happens all too often is that we give little attention to lots of things and effectively water down what should be our priorities.

This idea holds true for entire organizations as well and one of the best ways to get to the heart of what's holding you back is planning.

The first planning principle you must embrace, however, is that the goal of the process is to help you limit what you are going to do and do well. Instead of creating a laundry list of wants and dreams, your responsibility in the planning process is to create a very small list of objectives and goals grounded in the overriding purpose of the business. From that small list you can carve out a requisite number of strategies and tactics that support these business objectives.

In fact, your aim is to create a total plan outline that fills no more than one sheet of paper (six-point font allowed).

## The Hierarchy of Planning

There is always more that you want to do than you can humanly do. That's just the nature of owning a business, and the minute you let up, it comes right back at you.

The key is to find a way to focus on the right things and let the other things, no matter how loud and shiny, go.

The trouble is that in the course of a week, a day, or even an hour, what's important work and what's a distraction can look pretty much the same unless you have a plan—a plan for knowing what's important, a plan for what's now, and a plan for what's next.

While this may sound like a to-do list, and perhaps there is an element of that in it, it's much more than that. It's actually a strategy that begins with a clear understanding about what's pulling you forward, what's on the horizon, what's your target, what's the next hill, and what's on tap for the day.

## Hierarchy of Work

There is a hierarchy of work that must ebb and flow throughout your days and weeks that acts as the filter for your focus. This hierarchy has to inform what you allow yourself to do and not do throughout your week.

You can focus on only so many things, and if you are to move your business forward in a way that doesn't feel like treading water, you've got to focus on the right things.

**BAI.** At the top of the pyramid is what I call your one big audacious idea. This is the one thing that is far out there, but that possesses a gravitational pull that keeps you going. It's the big thing you know you want your business to become, even if you're not really sure today how you'll get there.

I believe you must always take stock of this idea and make sure it's alive and, in some cases, actually big enough to alter your behavior. Without this pull, the other stages can turn into busywork.

**Priorities.** Each year you should define your top three to four priorities. Keep this list small or your focus will become diluted. Most businesses can't accomplish more than this number and trying to do so means nothing really gets accomplished. This is also a great way to identify the highest payoff work when it comes down to utilizing scarce resources like the owner's time.

When you pare down your list to only the top priorities, you have a device for making determinations about what projects or great new ideas should actually receive consideration going forward. If they don't support one of your annual priorities, they go on the back burner for later consideration. It's a great way to keep everyone moving in the same direction, including the self-sabotaging owner!

**Goals.** Everyone is familiar with the idea of using goals, but few businesses establish goals as a key way to track and measure progress, particularly as it relates to the stated major priorities for the year.

After you agree upon the three to four priority objectives, you must establish goals that allow you to track your progress in ways that help you understand what's working and what's not.

**Projects.** Each of your priorities will involve any number of projects. For example, if one of your primary objectives for the year is to increase revenue by X percent, you'll probably need to identify a series of projects that are geared toward reaching that objective. This might include a new product launch or aggressive lead generation campaign.

You should attempt to identify only a handful of ongoing projects that support your main objectives on a quarter-by-quarter basis. These projects should have owners and supporters and progress should be tracked and reported on a weekly basis.

**Tasks.** The smallest unit of work is the task. Even so, tasks should be associated with projects, which in turn support the primary objectives.

Now, tasks often pop up in the form of the daily to-do list. People fail in their day-to-day productivity because many don't use to-do lists and those who do employ them don't always have the end in mind when they plan.

The hierarchy of important stuff suggests that unless you plan with the end in mind, or with a focus on the big audacious idea, you'll constantly fall victim to the swirl of what seems important at the time.

When you build your pyramid from the top down, you can plan your days, weeks, and months with each of the stages firmly rooted in every decision you make hour by precious hour.

## The Cycle of Getting Important Things Done

Staying focused on priorities is one of the toughest jobs we all have.

I outlined the path for staying focused above; now I want to address just how you stay on that path.

There are lots of time management systems out there, and the method I'm about to outline was developed by cobbling together parts of systems from some terribly genuine and creative people like Dan Sullivan of The Strategic Coach and David Allen of GTD. I've had the pleasure of spending time with both and credit them with a great deal of my thinking on managing myself.

The basic unit of my time and energy management tool that makes up this system path is the week.

I divide up each week into days with a specific type of work plan. Each type of day plan has a unique emphasis that is biased toward a certain type of work. I have Intention Days, Attention Days, and Ascension Days.

Intention Days are set aside to concentrate on my big ideas, my own personal growth, and in some cases renewal. I take my higher purpose into these days and allow myself the luxury of dreaming.

At the risk of getting too personal, these are days where I often spend a lot of time alone and reassess meetings and feelings and words I've used wisely and unwisely. These are days when I forgive myself and forgive others. This type of renewal allows me to tap that little flicker of creativity that I so often attempt to extinguish.

While I intentionally protect my thoughts and actions on these days, I don't go as far as banning all digital activity; I simply make certain that I witness my thoughts and spend time doing things I wouldn't normally do. I go to art museums and read books about architecture and geometry.

Attention Days are set aside to spend as much time as possible making money. Now, this may sound a little too focused for some, but what I really do is spend time doing my three or four highest-payoff activities. The kind of stuff that either makes me money now or lays the foundation for meeting objectives down the road.

For me, that's writing, creating products or courses, working with sponsors and customers, or writing an e-mail that entices people to sign up for a workshop.

I typically plan these days with my staff during our weekly all-hands meeting and take them outside the office to limit the temptation to stray from full attention.

These days are easy to plan, as I limit them to just a few items. In some cases, I may only get to creating a PowerPoint deck and writing one article, but I know it's the right work and I know it's time well spent.

Ascension Days are days spent climbing the hill. It's when I get to those meetings, interviews, WordPress Plugin tweaks, accounting reviews, in-box-emptying parties, and pretty much everything else screaming in my ear.

Maybe one day I'll get to the point where I never have these kinds of days, but I doubt it. Ascension Days are like physical therapy; you've got to do this work so you can grow and get to the high-payoff work.

All of these types of days, in fact, all of this type of work, is important, but my experience tells me that if you don't carve out and make time and space to dream and create and focus on priorities, every day will turn into a climb-the-hill day of stirring the noise.

My pattern for these days can change depending upon what's going on around me, but I typically try to take one Intention and two Attention Days a week and it's the thing that keeps me most sane.

## Committed Productivity

The first step in the process involves the owner of the business or perhaps the owner of the plan. The idea here is that if you are going to recalculate your focus and manage and delegate certain aspects of the plan, you need to be very clear first on where you fit in in the overall plan.

There are three things you need to spend some time determining before you can move the committed planning process out to your team.

## Figure Out the Things You Can't Do

I know that you have lots of answers. Your problem, and the problem with most business owners, is that nobody is asking you the right questions.

One of the questions you need to ask yourself and then answer honestly is why some things never seem to get done. So often the answer to this question is that there are things you simply can't do well.

The great thing about acknowledging these things is that most of the time they are also things that you don't enjoy trying to do. This simple acceptance can allow you to fully engage in finding team members and providers who excel at these things.

Figure out the things you won't do. Lots of people know what they should do; what's good for them and what's prudent. The problem all too often is that left alone, they do what feels good in the moment, what makes the most noise or strokes their ego.

That's why we're overweight, stressed, and burned out.

You must understand where you need to be held accountable, either by a coach, consultant, employee, mentor, or adviser, and give them the permission to hold you to your commitments.

## Figure Out the Things You Shouldn't Do

Spend some time analyzing where your company makes its money. You might find this is a pretty eye-opening exercise. When they stop and think about it, many business owners realize that their income is derived in a couple of thirty-minute blasts during the course of the day.

Let me ask you this. If given the opportunity to identify only three of your highest-payoff activities, what would be on that list?

Now, let me ask you something else. How much time do you spend doing those three activities and what would happen to your business if you spent twice as much time doing them?

Armed with your thoughts from the previous few sections, go to your note-taking page and record the three (and only three) highest-payoff ways for you to spend your time. Be very specific and thoughtful with this list, because it's going to be a key checkpoint for your entire planning process.

Meeting objectives, setting goals, and infusing your business with commitment is going to depend on your committing to do more of these three things, so take your time on this.

This list will be different for everyone, different for every kind of business, and certainly different depending upon the stage of business you find yourself in.

If your goal is to double your business in the next year, you know you'll probably need to find a way to do a lot more of the things on that short list while either delegating or deleting altogether some of the things that keep you juggling rather than focusing.

Dan Sullivan, founder of Strategic Coach, tells all of his clients about a baseball slugger who was paid an enormous amount of money for something that actually took him all of about two hours a year to do; he was paid about $5 million a year for the result of about forty at-bats or home runs.

Of course, he spent lots of time preparing, practicing, and rejuvenating, but home-run hitters make their money hitting home runs. So, what are your home runs?

# The Planning Process

Now let's move to a tool that you can use to create a much bigger plan for your fully alive business.

Most everyone who has ever made a business plan has used some mix of strategies, objectives, goals, tasks, constraints, priorities, and tactics.

The trick, of course, is to create a hierarchy of sorts so that each element supports the other. That is to say, a tactic is related to achieving a strategy that will help you reach a stated goal that would suggest the accomplishment of the plan objectives.

The key to creating a good plan, however, is to accept that there can never be more than three or four driving objectives.

As you'll soon see, a planning process like this can help create the kind of simple clarity that is so often missing in the "what should we do next" business management style.

Using these concepts, we're going to move to creating your very own committed planning document. This is a great exercise to do with key team members and certainly everyone in the organization should be taught how to use the tools described in this chapter as they begin to adopt their own planning, projects, and processes.

## The Committed Planning Workshop

Set aside an entire day for this process and think seriously about moving off-site to a location that will free people to be creative and detach from their normal roles.

Make your planning space a mobile- and laptop-free space. (You'll take breaks, but no checking e-mail during your sessions.)

In fact, since most firms use so much technology, switching to pencils, paper, markers, crayons, and sticky notes can be a great way to stimulate latent creativity.

Also, consider bringing in a facilitator, someone who knows your business well enough to keep things moving, but not so well as to place barriers. The problem with making this a CEO-run exercise is that you may unknowingly constrict brainstorming and in the role of facilitator fail to apply your own insights.

If you're the owner of the business, you will likely have some definite ideas about the strategic direction of the organization, but this is a group, composed at the very least of senior management, and in some organizations, an all-hands exercise.

So, let's get started, but first, the rules:

- Don't assume your normal roles.
- Let brainstorming happen.
- Be present and focused.
- Save judgment for tomorrow.
- Plan for the entire year.

And then some suggested requirements:

- Food and drink should be awesome.
- Leave lots of time and space for physical movement.
- Make it easy to capture everything.

Add the following A–G heading words to a deck of blank pages. For example, page one simply says "Objectives" at the top and the next page would say "Goals," and so on. Every participant gets a deck for brainstorming.

Start each section with a definition and perhaps some examples from your business.

### A. Objectives

At the very top of the planning process is a very small list of objectives. This list should end up being no more than three or four. These are organization-wide objectives, but from these, some individual departmental objectives may be developed as well.

The reason to limit this to no more than three or four is that few organizations can maintain the focus required to do more. As you'll see shortly, each objective will create its own list of strategies, tactics, and relevant projects.

The trick here is to think bigger, be realistic, and prioritize. If you are conducting this process as part of an overall annual planning process, don't get caught up in trying to do too much.

### B. Goals

These are the things you'll use to measure your progress toward achieving your objectives. So, for example, if one of your objectives is to increase brand awareness during the year, your charge here would be to set goals for measuring the increase in brand awareness.

Any measurement goal generally assumes that you have a baseline to start with, but don't let a lack of past data surrounding an objective stop you from creating goals.

You'll have a chance during the strategies and tactics sections to make sure you address your tracking process.

Each objective should receive at least one goal and some may have several.

### C. The Pivot Point

Many times organizations will carve out a set of objectives but stall when it comes time to create the actual strategies and tactics needed in order to achieve them. In some cases, this comes about because the people creating the objectives and the people creating the actual strategies and tactics to make them happen aren't the same people or aren't on the same page.

I find that by adding a step where you review the payoff involved in meeting an objective and, in addition, as you'll see in the next step, hashing out a few of the hurdles or constraints different staff members might pose, you are more suited to come up with strategies that are solutions the entire team can live with.

The problem with boldly or blindly creating objectives that sound good without enough consideration to the results and challenges each presents is that they can actually do harm and cause frustration rather than acting as a device to pull the team along.

With careful consideration of results comes greater leverage to find a solution and with careful vetting of constraints comes the reason why something is a good idea and how the team can solve the constraint together.

### D. Results

For each objective, make an attempt to clarify the result or payoff that achieving the objective will cause. The idea is to paint as clear a picture as possible of what this is going to mean to the organization.

So, for example, if an objective is to accomplish something along the lines of "increase brand awareness," some payoffs might be making it easier to get sales appointments, increasing media exposure, and putting more leads in the top of the funnel.

Create as many specific results as possible and let each department tap into the results that might be specific to them. The more results you can identify, the more buy-in you'll get from the team.

### E. Constraints

Constraints are a friendly way of noting objections or hurdles. One of the things I often encounter when working with firms on strategies and objectives is that various members of the leadership team can't get past why something won't work thoroughly enough to get behind any sort of unified plan.

In some cases there are legitimate reasons why a properly stated constraint can effectively derail an objective and get everyone behind eliminating it from the plan at least for now, but more often than not, constraints give everyone a common point to attack when trying to determine strategies that will help eliminate or overcome the hurdles.

By giving a voice to the constraints and airing why something won't work, you encourage a team approach to get behind how to make it work.

## F. Strategies

Now, *strategy* is one of the most abused words in the business lexicon. I've used it to define several things just in this book, and we could take a quick trip online and probably uncover several hundred definitions and uses.

For this planning process, I use the word *strategy* to house a set of tactics aimed at achieving one or more of our stated objectives.

Each objective can have more than one strategy (although probably no more than three) and each strategy will likely have a number of associated tactics needed to carry it out.

So, returning to my example of increasing brand awareness as an objective, one might state "create a listening station" as a strategy with the goal of monitoring the brand mentions and reputation.

## G. Tactics

A *tactic* is probably the most comfortable planning term for most business owners, as it is very task-oriented. In fact, one of the challenges most people face when going through this process is to guard against making everything a tactic.

Many times what people call a strategy, and even an objective, is really a tactic. Always ask yourself if something in your plan is really just a task.

As stated above, each strategy will likely be accompanied by a list or set of tactics, so once you get your strategies honed down to no more than three or four per objective, it's time to propose tactics that people will act on.

Remember, this is just the planning process so that you can create the one-page plan. We'll address who, what, when, and where in the next section.

And finally, our "create a listening station strategy" might have related tactics such as "identify list of monitoring terms," "source vendor or tool to employ," and "create listening dashboard."

### The One-Page Plan

Now take your objectives, goals, strategies, and tactics and align them on one page each in support of the proper top-line objective.

When used in conjunction with the statement of your higher purpose and committed beliefs, this document will become the most important tool your organization has for day-to-day alignment and focus.

# 14

# Managing Committed Work

**Planning, as we've covered in** the last chapter, is a tremendous way to create clarity, focus, and purposeful objectives for an entire year, but at some point your plans must be broken down into bite-size chunks and even daily routines.

In this chapter, we'll explore a few processes needed to keep the work infused with purpose and managed in a way that truly empowers every employee to take action.

I know people toss the word *empower* around lightly and with little thought as to what it really means. To me, it simply means that people know what to do and how to do it and have permission to do it the best way possible.

Few things are more disempowering than being put in a position where you are forced to wait around for someone to tell you what to do next. While some organizations may have roles that are, by nature, mostly process-oriented, every staff member should understand where they fit into the organization's objectives and how they will be held accountable for results.

It's a little like saying if you want someone to get good at playing a game, they must know the rules and how to win; otherwise, they will get very bored, very fast.

The following processes make up the framework for work flow, responsibility, accountability, and communication that will provide the fertile ground for your purpose-based culture to grow.

Remember, however, that these are simply tools that help create structure and a common language; your passion, purpose, and core values must still be front and center at all times.

## How the Plan Gets Done

The next tool in the committed planning process is something called RACI.

RACI is an acronym for the words *Responsible, Accountable, Consulted,* and *Informed.* This is how we take the one-page plan and get it distributed in a way that makes sure it gets done—or at least gets mapped out with that intention.

I certainly can't take credit for inventing this process, as it's a pretty commonly recognized method for organizing just about any project or business alignment and is chronicled in dozens of books and methodologies on management.*

The idea here is that we are going to go through each tactic in your one-page plan from the last chapter and determine and assign the roles and project plans for each one, creating a grid of projects.

This is how you'll map out getting the work done and on track with the greatest amount of buy-in and understanding.

## First, the RACI Definitions

> **Responsible (R):** This is the person or function that is ultimately responsible for the results. This person may not do the work, but this is where the buck stops when things go right or wrong.

---

* J. Mike Jacka and Paulette J. Keller, *Business Process Mapping: Improving Customer Satisfaction* (New York: John Wiley and Sons, 2009), 257.

**Accountable (A):** This is the person or people or in some cases department or vendor who will be accountable for the actual work. This can be the same person as the (R), but it's often a person managed by the (R).

**Consulted (C):** In most organizations there will be people who need to be consulted before a task can be completed, either to sign off on a budget item or give input as to how to do something. These people will be assigned a (C) role in the grid.

**Informed (I):** The last category is reserved for those who simply need to be kept in the loop or reported to. This may be the owner or department head and be done via meeting or simply by way of e-mail updates.

While you can have multiple people or functions in some boxes, it's best to stick with one (R) for any tactic.

So, now it's time to go through your list of tactics from your one-page plan, group them by strategy, and assign people or functions to each according to the RACI definitions above.

This does not mean you will do each project or tactic simultaneously; it's simply a method for creating project teams and roles. As we'll discuss shortly, each team will create separate project plans.

# Creating Project Plans

Once the RACI is complete, you can begin to build specific plans for each project and perhaps break them down into even smaller tasks.

Some projects will be fairly complex, far-reaching, and involve moving parts. These kinds of projects really benefit from this degree of detail.

For organizations that are not used to this degree of planning and documentation, this can feel tedious at first, but in the long run it's how everyone stays engaged and focused on the right things.

Use judgment for those times when something may not require anything as elaborate as a plan; perhaps a tactic can be knocked out with a meeting. Just record the dates back on the RACI and move on.

Resist the urge to dismiss this step as creativity-killing paperwork. When everyone is working with project plans, schedules, and expectations, it actually frees you to be more creative because you know steps are being taken and the right people have accepted responsibility.

Project plans free everyone to do their best work and eliminate a great deal of the waste associated with managing tasks and people.

You complete a project plan in two important steps:

1. Fill in the various tasks and dates.
2. Put milestone dates on the RACI.

Create a spreadsheet with the figure below as a guide and then break the project down into smaller tasks to make it easier to schedule resources and complete chunks. You may find that it's a good idea to add things like start and finish dates so that others who may need to access the project or depend upon the completion of a task in order to move another project forward can schedule accordingly.

I can't overemphasize the freedom this kind of planning brings once everyone is using the same language.

## Online Tools

There are a number of very powerful online applications that can be employed in the same manner as the project plan described here. Many firms use tools such as Basecamp from 37signals (basecampHQ.com) or Mavenlink to create and manage projects, assign tasks, and communicate progress.

The key is to fit these tools into an overall planning platform that everyone uses. The best tool for the job is often the one that everyone can learn and will actually use. Don't scrap the process because you get resistance when you introduce a new tool, technology, or process.

Remember, this isn't simply a management process; this is a culture-building and commitment-generating process at heart because it puts your people in control and keeps them focused on the right work.

# Accountability Meetings

Scheduled communication may be one of the most powerful culture-building tools available when done the right way.

However, there are two very commonly abused meeting methods that you should avoid at all costs.

One is the "I hate meetings, so just come to me if you have a problem" method. Of course this is quite possibly the most frustrating approach for all concerned. This approach leads to lots of wasted time and the every-ten-minute-or-so interruption.

The other approach is what I refer to as the "I've called a meeting, but it's really a reading" approach. In this approach, managers read from a list of to-dos that could have been sent via e-mail and then propose some things to try to get buy in on.

This second approach eventually leads to the "I hate meetings" attitude and drains any sense of commitment from all involved.

Here's the deal: you need meetings, perhaps frequently, but you need them to be energetic, useful, and, in the words of consultant Al Pittampalli, *modern*.

In *Read This Before Our Next Meeting*, Pittampalli lists the seven attributes of what he calls the modern meeting.* This is a great framework for how to think about meetings that generate commitment.

1. The Modern Meeting supports a decision that has already been made.
2. The Modern Meeting starts on time, moves fast, and ends on schedule.
3. The Modern Meeting limits the number of attendees.

* Al Pittampalli, *Read This Before Our Next Meeting*, The Domino Project, August 3, 2011.

**4.** The Modern Meeting rejects the unprepared.

**5.** The Modern Meeting produces committed action plans.

**6.** The Modern Meeting refuses to be informational. Reading memos is mandatory.

**7.** The Modern Meeting works only alongside a culture of brainstorming.

Read Pittampalli's book before your next meeting and consider making it a gift to everyone in your organization.

To keep commitment high and to reinforce a culture based on core values and purpose, you need to install a systematic approach to meetings that allows people to be heard, get help, pose ideas, participate, learn, grow, move projects forward, and stay connected.

This will include annual, quarterly, monthly, weekly, and even daily planned sessions designed to accomplish specific tasks.

I can almost hear some collective groaning coming from my readers, but trust me on this. If you do this right, you'll wonder how you ever succeeded without it. You may find that more gets done in terms of actual work and real team building in a month using this system than at any other time in your business.

First off, have everyone in the organization sketch out their near-term plans. The projects they need or intend to get done in thirty, sixty, and ninety days. This should be an ongoing moving process and will be one of the tools used in your meeting system.

## Daily, Weekly, Monthly, and Quarterly

Every organization, depending upon the number of employees and other logistics, will have slightly differing needs, but the basic framework should look something like this:

**Quarterly meetings.** These meetings should be used to give "state-of-the-business updates" that will likely include financial data and reporting on goals and objectives for the year.

One of the ways that many organizations reinforce core values is to choose a quarterly theme that relates to one of their stated core values and plan activities and initiatives that highlight the chosen value. I'll go into more detail about this specific tactic in a subsequent chapter on culture.

These meetings should be fun and should celebrate achievements, milestones, and accomplishments that may fall outside the realm of work.

**Monthly meetings**. These meetings may include financial and milestone reporting, but should also include teaching.

One of my favorite ways to include teaching in the monthly meeting is to select a member of the staff, regardless of department, and charge them with leading a session about their department or function's specific initiatives, goals, and achievements.

This can be a fun way to "get to know accounting" or "showcase the new advertising campaign."

**Weekly functional meetings.** It gets a little trickier once you start breaking meetings down to functional teams or departments. This is where organizations with flat structures (everyone reports to one boss) start to choke. If you're the boss and you manage everyone in the organization, this tactic will reveal why you can't continue this practice.

The good news is that this process and the "Committed Planning Workshop" process outlined in the previous chapter are how you start to create a management structure in your organization where perhaps none existed previously.

In fact, many organizations find that the sheer act of planning as described in this book creates its own logical team organization structure based on who can be and is responsible for projects. I'll end this chapter with more on that topic, but what about the weekly meetings?

The focus of this meeting is project movement. If you have a very small staff, this may be a weekly staff meeting, but the focus is still to get updates on projects. If you have a very large or geographically dispersed organization you may logically conduct these in small groups around projects.

Some midsize organizations hold weekly all-hands meetings in addition to functional staff meetings in an effort to highlight their most important initiatives.

VML, a digital marketing agency located in Kansas City, holds an all-staff meeting every Tuesday morning with the primary purpose of highlighting the organization's community, nonprofit, and charitable activities. The brief meeting is also frequently used as a way to recognize staff members who exemplified core values during the course of the week.

**Daily functional huddle.** The concept of the daily huddle has been used in large businesses for years and has had a huge impact on organizations such as Ritz-Carlton, Johnson & Johnson, and 3M. Verne Harnish, author of *Mastering the Rockefeller Habits,* did a great deal to popularize the notion in small-business circles. Harnish contends that this was one of the core concepts Rockefeller used while building Standard Oil.

While some may view this tactic purely in terms of efficiency, I think it's one of the greatest ways to build team commitment and spirit and once again reinforce purpose.

The idea is pretty simple.

Every morning at nine-fifteen, the leadership team at Appletree Answers gathers for a standing fifteen-minute meeting (literally standing as opposed to sitting around a table) in which each member will share information about their number one priority or objective, anything they are stuck on, and information that pertains to their core values.

In a recent meeting, a manager shared information about an employee in need and the team immediately determined that pitching in and helping was very much in line with their core value of taking care of their employees.

Once a day, preferably early in the day, a small company or team huddles for no more than fifteen minutes (some organizations call these stand-up or lineup meetings to emphasize the short time period).

The agenda may vary from organization to organization but

should remain the same each day for your organization. This way people get familiar with the routine.

This is not a problem-solving session; it's a check-in, so you must be pretty vigilant about keeping to the agenda.

A typical daily huddle agenda may go as follows:

- Right Now: This is less than a minute of what we are working on right now.
- Key Numbers: This is a report of whatever metrics are important to your work.
- Challenges: This is the "Ask for help" or "Here's where we are stuck" section.
- Values: This is the "Here's a great compliment we received" or "Here's something you need to know about a core value in action" section.

Give these daily meetings a structure and stick to them. Once people start to get the hang of them, they will become easier to run and more productive.

One of the things that many people find is that all these meetings actually lead to fewer meetings and certainly to fewer interruptions throughout the workday.

Planning and meetings alone aren't enough to create and foster an environment of commitment. Many organizations go to great lengths to live a culture where purpose and commitment grow, but the framework outlined in this chapter is central to creating a common focus so that everyone is engaged in meaningful work and pulling in the same direction.

# 15

# Patterns of Committed Teaching

**How everyone in the organization** learns, develops, and nurtures commitment is an intentional act. Fully alive organizations go to work on the advancement of their staff much in the way that a school might develop someone in a degree program.

Developing your people comes not only from establishing great teaching programs but also from a commitment to teaching and learning as a way of doing business.

We're always learning, whether we think so or not—even in those moments when we think what we're doing is teaching.

For even when we are explaining something, lecturing, training, teaching, speaking, or managing—if we're present while doing these things—we're actually learning how to do all of these things better.

There are times in my life when I've felt as though I was enduring a lesson from someone who was telling me how to do something that I clearly knew how to do (or thought I did)—perhaps better than they.

When I look back at these times through the learning lens, I now see that not only was I learning an important lesson, but the person conveying the lesson was also learning how to better communicate. I'm going to take that lesson into every meeting I attend going forward.

I think there's an immediate message in this for business owners. Every moment is really both a learning moment and a teaching moment, and we've got to start viewing it that way.

Businesses with strong brand-supporting cultures use this notion to intentionally infuse the business with life.

Nobody is born knowing how to run a business. We are always learning how to run our own businesses. Our managers are always learning how to manage. Our staff is always engaged in learning how to operate process. Even those charged with teaching are learners.

And that's how we need to think about the people in our businesses. Below are three simple ways to make learning moments part of the everyday culture of your business.

## Teaching

Every employee should be given the task of teaching something to someone as a matter of course. It could be teaching members of another department how something is done. It could be running the all-hands meeting to present the new advertising campaign. It could be outlining the mission of a not-for-profit partner the firm might help.

Everyone should be asked to teach because that's how we learn best.

## Mentoring

Once a week every employee should have a thirty-minute one-on-one meeting with their manager where the employee owns the agenda 100 percent.

The meeting could be the opportunity to figure out how to do something that is holding up a project, or it could be the chance to outline a pet project the employee would like to take on, or it could simply be the time to explore their life goals.

Managers learn how to manage when they learn about the people they are managing.

### Planned Learning

Once a week gather your team or department over lunch and just share. Invite a new person to play host each week and challenge them to make the session fun. This can be a formal session or people can just talk about whatever they want, but everyone must participate.

You can share facts about yourself, teach about a quick subject unrelated to work, or read a poem that means something to you.

These weekly sessions are how you discover what everyone really cares about and that's how you learn how to make the organization special. That's how you generate commitment. That's how this buzzword culture really comes to life—from the little, seemingly insignificant things we learn while trying to teach one another.

# The Art of Perceptive Listening

Listening is a skill that all business owners, marketers, and managers must develop. Or, perhaps more accurately, redevelop.

Most people are born with the ability to hear and, over time, interpret what's being said. Somewhere along the line we get so consciously competent at hearing that we no longer feel the need to listen.

I believe that one of the master skills of any marketer, manager, or educator is the ability to listen perceptively to what our prospects, customers, staff, and community members are saying. And I further believe this is something we all have to work at.

So, what is perceptive listening?

People who teach this sort of thing might say there are many forms of listening.

- Passive listening: the kind we do when we are listening to a seminar but we're really scrolling through Pinterest.
- Selective listening: the kind that I might practice when I'm discussing something with someone and mostly I'm thinking about what I'm going to say next.
- Active listening: the kind where we are discussing something with someone and reacting only to the words being said.
- Perceptive listening: the kind where I hear and interpret the words, but I also consider what the person is thinking and perhaps how they are acting as they say the words.

Perceptive listening is by far the most complex because it requires you to be totally focused, completely mindful, and aware of what's really going on.

Perceptive listening is also something the party being listened to can feel. We've all grown pretty numb to conversing with people while they divide their attention between our words and their iPhone.

Perceptive listening is how you tell when a prospect says they're not ready to buy, but what they are really saying is they don't understand the benefits.

Perceptive listening is how you mentor an employee. It's how you draw out what they are truly passionate about. It's how you help them self-manage and lead.

I believe you can even use perceptive listening to monitor the things you say to yourself. When you are mindful enough to stop and witness your own thoughts and perceive how they truly make you feel, your actions will be much more informed.

Effective listening can be learned and takes practice. It's a habit of sorts, just like multitasking is a habit.

Below are several exercises that I challenge you to undertake in an effort first to experience your level of perceptive listening and then to bring this art front and center in everything you do.

## Listening to a Client

Make a list of five clients you respect and would like to understand better. Set a time to sit down with them and ask them these three questions. Make certain that you give their answers your full attention and pay close attention to how they answer, including their body language.

**1.** What's the one thing you love about what we do?
**2.** If you referred us to a friend, what would you say?
**3.** What's the biggest challenge you have in your business right now?

## Listening to a Staff Member

This time choose a member of your staff whom you would like to develop further and start with these questions.

**1.** What's the one thing you love most about coming to work here?
**2.** If you referred us to a friend, what would you say?
**3.** What's the biggest challenge you have in meeting your objectives right now?

## Listening to Yourself

This might be the toughest act yet, but sit down and ponder these questions posed to yourself and pay attention to how you feel about the answers. You aren't really looking for right or wrong answers, you're merely checking for cracks in the alignment.

**1.** What's the one thing you love most about what you do?

**2.** Why do you really do what you do?

**3.** If you could do anything you wanted, would this be it?

## Listening to Music

Put on a piece of instrumental music. (If you're looking for a suggestion, you can't go wrong with a Bach cello suite.) Close your eyes and try to focus on the rests and spaces *between* the notes. Listen keenly for what musicians refer to as grace notes, the little half-played notes that flick inside a pause or occur between the beats.

This is a completely different way to listen to music and I think it can help tune your sensitivity to the art of listening to the complete story.

You can't have art or music without this negative space and I think the same is true when it comes to perceptive listening.

## Listening in Space

Another exercise I love to do is to sit somewhere in a room and close my eyes. Once I kind of empty my thoughts, I start actively listening for the sounds right around me—the water running in the pipes, the printer, a stereo playing.

Next I try to move my listening out farther, to focus on the street sounds—the cars passing by, the construction work across the street, people coming and going.

Finally, I try to move my listening out as far as I can. Through this targeted listening, I can perceive an airplane overhead and a train slowly rumbling through another part of town.

Some of the exercises above might seem like odd ways to get better at managing or marketing, but generating commitment is often about listening to and understanding what's really going on all around you.

## Passion and Purpose Workshops

John Ratliff of Appletree Answers attended a program based on Gazelles' founder Verne Harnish's book *Mastering the Rockefeller Habits*.

He was so taken by the program that he returned to the office full of ideas, plans, and initiatives. Even with the force of his enthusiasm, Ratliff's new business-building strategies failed to fully inspire and motivate his staff as he had hoped.

It was only when he decided to invest in sending his entire leadership team to the program that the ideas began to take root. He still firmly believes in formal development programs and his company invests tens of thousands of dollars in staff development every year.

While external or formal programs that are aligned with your core values can play a big part in helping to develop your team, you should also invest in the creation of internal programs that can be used to expose your entire team to the tools covered early on in this work aimed at helping them gain access to a sense of individual passion and purpose.

What if you were to help your staff members discover more about themselves and their passions in much the same way I asked you to learn about yourself at the beginning of this journey?

What if you created internal mentoring programs and paired new employees with "sponsors" or mentors?

It's important to schedule regular sessions and to help your staff create goals that inspire them to take more ownership, responsibility, and accountability.

## Employee-Generated Content

Some of the most authentic content and storytelling comes from your staff and customers. Capturing video of staff members telling it like it is or sharing their personal story of triumph, pain, passion, purpose, inspiration, or even just flat-out fun is a great way to make a point that might otherwise fall flat in the typical corporate training video.

Education that features your staff and customers is a very powerful way to build a library of content that feels more like sharing than training. It's also a great way to demonstrate the core values in action.

On a trip to Texas, I had the chance to tour Dell Computer's Social Media Listening Command Center. The center tracks, on average, more than twenty-two thousand daily topic posts related to Dell, as well as mentions of Dell on Twitter, and that information is analyzed and broken down based on topics and subjects of conversation, sentiment, share of voice, geography, and trends.

According to Dell, one of the primary reasons to track all this information is to get it in the hands of the people most capable of providing the best response. In order to make this work, Dell created a voluntary employee-training program called Social Media and Community University, or SMaC University.

All employees, regardless of function, are encouraged to join the program, complete the training, and get certified in order to participate in social media conversations on behalf of Dell.

I asked Amy Fowler-Tennison, Dell's SMaC University program lead, about how employees get certified.

"There are two levels of certification: SMaC professional and SMaC spokesperson. Professional certification requires basic understanding of four main content areas: our SMaC principles, Dell's overarching social media strategy, how to represent the brand in social media, and governance for the platform they choose to use. Spokesperson certification requires additional media training since these team members are using social media to communicate to shareholders and media."

The program has been so successful that at the time of my tour several thousand Dell employees had completed the training and were engaging customers and creating content on behalf of the brand. More important, during an initial start-up phase of the program, Dell saw a 30 percent drop in negative comments in social media.

Employees are acting as brand ambassadors and this kind of "employee branding" goes a long way toward attracting both staff and customers who can clearly witness the culture and beliefs in action.

## The Committed Handbook

Most companies invest in employee handbooks. These valuable resources detail rules, regulations, mission statements, policies, and expected conduct. But they often ignore what might be the most important company knowledge—marketing.

Any employee who comes into contact with a customer or client is performing a marketing function. Do they know how to represent the organization accurately and positively?

Business owners should add marketing training to the ongoing development of every staff member. Teach new hires and conduct routine, perhaps quarterly, all-hands sessions.

Here are the seven things to work into training your staff in marketing.

### 1. This is whom we work with.

Write a paragraph that paints a vivid picture of the kind of client you seek to serve. Include the problems or challenges that make your company the right one for them to do business with.

Until you narrowly define the exact person or business that is your ideal client (or problem that client has), your business will fall prey to the marketing tactic of the week.

### 2. This makes us unique.

Give your staff a simple yet compelling way to introduce what your firm does that's unique. This is your core marketing message. It communicates why your product or service produces greater value than every other option.

Have employees practice this by role-playing until they are comfortable delivering it authentically.

### 3. This is what our clients worry about.

People rarely walk around saying they need your product or service. But they do lament the lack of something. They talk about specific problems or voice an aspiration.

Instead of saying "I wish I had some new accounting software," they say things like "I can't ever get a handle on my receivables."

Your entire staff should know the most common things people say that indicate they could be an ideal prospect.

### 4. This is how we keep our brand true.

Your marketing department probably spends time and money on getting the color and font of your marketing materials just right. But everyone else in the business just wings it in their communications. If employees don't practice consistency, how will your clients recognize your brand?

The best way to adhere to brand standards is to make them internal as well as external. Train everyone on the use of color, type, and images and demand that they adhere to these standards in their communications. This will ensure that everyone is consistent with the visual elements of your marketing.

### 5. This is what we are saying right now.

Show off your latest ads, mock-ups for the next direct-mail piece, and offers that are going out in every medium. Make sure that your entire staff can talk about your current promotions.

When your staff is not able to comfortably answer questions about what is going on with your business, it's bad for your company. Keeping them in the loop will make them feel even more engaged in marketing. It will also give them the confidence to better serve your customers.

### 6. This is how we take care of our customers.

Make sure the entire staff reads the company blog, understands the educational content, attends your online training, and routinely takes a shift answering customer service calls. Have your staff view the content you produce from the client's perspective.

### 7. This is how we all win.

Give your staff a way to know if the company is winning the game. Share the key strategic indicators your organization uses to measure success. Teach them what these indicators mean and help them find a way to tie what they do to one or more of these numbers.

If every employee realizes the way their day-to-day contribution adds to a key indicator of success, and ultimately to the overall success of the organization, you give them a way to connect everything they do with success.

With this understanding, they know that cutting costs in their department can contribute to lowering the client-acquisition cost.

Every business is a marketing business, and all employees trained this way can become contributing members of the marketing team, no matter what their job title is.

# 16

# Staff as Owner

**I believe that one of** the greatest opportunities we have as business owners is to create wealth.

By that I don't necessarily mean getting wealthy. I mean creating an asset, a business, that is worth more today than it was yesterday. All too often this view gets buried in the push to create a paycheck.

In my view, there are much easier ways to draw a salary than owning a business.

The real magic when you view your business as a tool to create wealth comes when you also see it as a way to create wealth for all the people who work to increase the market value of the business.

The key to this notion is shared ownership.

Sharing ownership with employees has become much more popular in the world of Internet start-ups and IPOs. The idea is that if people have stock, they'll be more productive.

The problem with this mentality, however, is that if employees don't have what could be called "psychic ownership" first and foremost, real ownership by way of stock options probably won't benefit anyone.

Psychic ownership suggests a culture where employees feel like owners, act like owners, and think like owners, even though they may not actually have any formal equity in the company.

The fact is, many companies try to explore this idea of shared ownership but approach it in name only.

If employees don't feel like they have a stake in what happens, don't have access to the financial data, or can't make decisions that impact the value of their ownership, then all the stock options in the world won't help. In fact, organizations that simply adopt an ownership or equity type of environment based on paper only find that it can be a disincentive and create entitlement without accountability.

Until you can create a culture that fosters psychic ownership first—a place where people feel empowered as owners, even if they're not—you'll never realize the benefits of providing real ownership.

The combination of a psychic ownership environment and real ownership structure, however, is perhaps the most potent tool for the creation of commitment that can be employed.

## Creating a Culture of Shared Ownership

A return to the Sky Factory's core beliefs may help illustrate ownership thinking taken to a level that defies traditional business building in almost every sense of the term.

When founder Bill Witherspoon, as he approached the age of sixty, determined that he would start yet another company, he sat back and analyzed his past failures and successes and concluded that he had never been very good at managing people or the organization once it had grown to a certain level.

So he decided to throw out everything he had ever done or learned about traditional management and start with a totally new view of how to build, in his words, a "beautiful corporation," also something of an oxymoron in his view.

Having a background in bioscience, he determined that every organization's DNA lies in the company culture and he knew he had to emphasize that element above all else. The company's core beliefs sprang from that thinking, but became much more than words on a lobby sign.

**Transparency.** Now there's a word that's been abused in business writing over the last few years, but taken at face value, and in this context, it simply means sharing everything with everyone in the company.

Jack Stack's *Great Game of Business* and *A Stake in the Outcome* have become the standard resources for how companies instill financial openness, reporting, and accountability, but the Sky Factory goes far beyond simply reporting financial metrics and shares every decision the company is involved in making.

Every Friday afternoon the entire staff gathers to go over the metrics one by one. Even things like how much cash is in the bank is reported. (The only metric that is not public is individual salaries.) Every department talks about goals and challenges and the entire team of forty can discuss any element that's shared.

When issues arise that need to be shared quickly, they call impromptu "stand-up" meetings and shut down all operations so that everyone can be involved.

If information is seen as power in business, then the Sky Factory believes in distributing that power.

**Autonomy.** There are no vice presidents, no managers, and no shop supervisors at the Sky Factory. If they had an organization chart, it would be very flat.

The company is organized into functional teams based on related work and each team uses a rotating facilitation model to keep things moving in place of the traditional manager.

Every week two members of a team take on the role of management. Everyone on the team takes a turn and Witherspoon feels that this concept allows people to learn, grow, and earn greater respect from other members of the staff.

This no-hierarchy approach removes politics and frees people to stretch far beyond the confines of the normal job description. The Sky Factory has numerous job descriptions that are tied to functional work that must be done, but the goal is to create a workplace where everyone can essentially do everything.

There certainly are instances where this isn't practical or possible, but no one gets tethered to one kind of work, no one gets bored, and everyone is asked to grow and given the opportunity to do work that continually stretches them.

The Sky Factory also finds that the experience creates built-in continuous improvement because new people are always able to provide a fresh approach by working new processes and systems.

**Consensus.** Every important decision made at the Sky Factory is made through a system of consensus. Some decisions are made at the departmental level, while others are discussed and determined by the company as a whole, but if there's even one person who can't say yes to a decision, it must be reevaluated.

Dissenters are asked to explain and own their no votes, and more often than not, the no simply leads to more research or looking at a decision in a new light, but everyone has a real voice in the process.

This process can take the form of a high-powered suggestion box as well. Many times when a decision needs to be made, the meeting that has been called to make the decision turns up suggestions that no one had considered.

Witherspoon tells a story about a time when the company determined that they were holding on to too much cash and wanted to decide what to do with it. He says the meeting had gone on for about half an hour with no real solid ideas bubbling up when an employee who at the moment was the youngest in age and the most recent hire spoke up and suggested that the company pay off the mortgage on its building.

The idea had not occurred to anyone else and years later, when many other companies suffered through a market recession, the Sky Factory was in much better shape operations-wise due to this decision that came about through consensus.

Here's another story about how consensus can impact operations. The company was experiencing a high percentage of late deliveries on promised projects. They had tried a number of process improvements to no avail. During one of their weekly meeting, an employee suggested that they should tie profit-sharing bonuses to delivery. The group agreed and the rule became that if even one delivery missed its promised date during a month, no one in the organization would receive that month's profit-sharing bonus.

Since the company adopted this rule several years ago, they virtually eliminated the problem. Everyone in the organization is now concerned about late deliveries and everyone is focused on pitching in and solving any potential snags in any part of the production process. And you can bet that if someone is having an issue with an order, they ask for help.

Witherspoon contends that this rule has actually enhanced teamwork and fostered an environment of greater mutual respect, although some people might think it would lead to finger-pointing and ill will. The key is the requirement of 100 percent consent.

Of course, consensus won't work if there's no transparency and truly no hierarchy. Consensus as a stand-alone tool is a recipe for disaster, but teamed with complete sharing of information and rotational management, it is the tool that turns everyone into an owner.

When an entrepreneur starts a business and it's just them, they have all the information, have no hierarchy, and get consensus on every decision. Shared ownership thinking simply takes this to another level.

## Performance-Based Ownership

There are many ways recognized by the IRS for a company to share real ownership with its employees: employee stock options, employee stock ownership plans, and employee stock purchase plans to name a few.

Employee stock options are the most commonly used form, but in recent years they've attracted criticism because they aren't accurately tied to performance and do little to foster ownership behavior.

I think the Sky Factory may have created an almost perfect formula for tying compensation and ownership to performance in a way that has every staff member watching the bottom line and serving customers in extraordinary ways.

## Profit Sharing

The Sky Factory places 50 percent of the profit from each month into a profit-sharing pool and compensates employees based on individual salary divided by total salary as soon as the books for the month are closed.

The impact of this step is dramatic. First and foremost it creates an environment of immediate feedback and immediate reward, but most importantly it creates an environment focused on performance.

Not only are employees encouraged to do great work, they are also encouraged to keep an eye on costs, on service, on one another, and to do it with as few people as possible.

Some might be tempted to suggest that this could lead to unstable performance if a team that needs to hire resists, but because performance includes delivery and service benchmarks, every department closely monitors when they need help and presents the idea for consensus.

The Sky Factory's profit-sharing plan also requires that the company has positive cash flow from operations for the last twelve weeks or there is no distribution. Since putting the plan in place over seven years ago, they have had only one instance where cash-flow issues disrupted profit sharing.

## Ownership Distribution

One of the great reasons to build a business is to build wealth. That's why profit is such an important marker of a fully alive business; without it, all you're left building is jobs.

True commitment comes when an organization can share the wealth or market value that is being built with the people who are responsible for building it.

The owner or founder of a business may have the brilliant idea that the business is built upon and may have had the instincts to get the business off the ground, but as I stated numerous times in this work, it's the ability to generate commitment in others that dictates the ultimate path of the business.

In that regard, there are loosely three groups of people that should be considered for performance-based ownership distribution—the founder(s), employees, and investors. (In many cases the latter won't be a part of the equation.)

The Sky Factory has created an innovative, and not terribly complicated, way to create wealth for all three parties based on true performance.

The first piece of the puzzle is market valuation. It's very difficult to distribute ownership unless there is an assessment of worth. Instead of determining today's worth, the Sky Factory established a value goal based on growth projections and the advice of investment firms.

Using this number, they established a formula of ownership upon reaching that market value goal. Founder 30 percent; investors 30 percent; and employees 40 percent.

After one full year of employment, every employee is offered the option to buy membership based upon their current individual salary. (The term *membership* is used for LLC as opposed to stock.)

The Sky Factory is able to discount the shares to 20 percent of their current value and loan the employee the money, through a long-term note, to purchase the shares out of profits. The net effect of this structure is that everyone wins if the company wins, everyone is rewarded fairly, and everyone has, borrowing a well-worn cliché, skin in the game.

Each paycheck has a small loan repayment deduction, reminding employees of the cost of ownership. This truly is a structure built on shared ownership, commitment, and performance that teaches value and wealth building as central themes throughout the organization.

Shared ownership is a crucial piece of *The Commitment Engine* approach, but it won't have the impact it should have if shared beliefs, plans, and goals aren't established first.

## Part 3

# The Promise:
# Community

# 17

# The Community Is the Business

**The work we've done in** the first two parts of this book has been a prelude to the ultimate expression of commitment—a loyal customer—or perhaps more broadly, a devoted community.

As I stated at the very beginning of this journey, I define *community* as anyone who comes into contact with your business—prospects, customers, journalists, suppliers, advisers, partners, and even competitors.

This is the place where some businesses that are fully alive stumble internally. What I'm going to ask you to do now is take passion and purpose and fully communicate it externally as position and personality in order to attract and engage a community that's committed to your business.

While this part of the book is devoted primarily to what will be seen as marketing relating to the customer, it is not a thorough discussion of how to approach marketing. For that, refer to my previous works, *Duct Tape Marketing* and *The Referral Engine*.

The goal of this final section is to help you take what you've gained by igniting your passion and purpose, injecting it into your organization's culture, and bringing it to the market in a strategic manner.

While there will be plenty of specific tactics, this section aims to address marketing and community building from a strategic point of view.

The meteoric rise of networks like Facebook and Google+ are a testament to the fact that people are drawn to the new form of community.

Online communities that give people the opportunity to join painlessly, come together around shared ideas, and engage and build deeper relationships based on value received represent the new business model.

In this chapter, we'll cover the basics of how to bring the community mind-set into your business, and subsequent chapters will dive deeply into the tactical elements required to live the community model inside and outside the business.

## Build Your Community Then Build Your Business

In a perfect world, every business would spend a year or so doing nothing but community building before they ever opened the doors.

What would that look like?

Natalie George had a day job and a dream of opening a healthy, all-natural, vegan and raw-food restaurant. The vision for this restaurant was created after dining at the well-known San Francisco restaurant Café Gratitude.

After several years of hoping and planning, she launched the business. The only thing is, there were no pots and pans or forks or glasses. In fact, there was no physical place at all. She launched the business by asking people to help her build it.

She began by inviting people to join a community that cared about the ideals of gratitude, abundance, community building, and, of course, raw food.

She raised money to build the business by holding workshops and selling gift cards for future use. She asked everyone to join her mailing list to keep up on the progress. She shared stories about the ups and downs, exciting and frustrating moments, and the joy of making tables from reclaimed wood.

The following four items were the focus of her Web site.

Café Gratitude is opening in Kansas City
    Would you like to be a part of making it happen?
There are several ways to contribute!
    1. We are starting Café Gratitude KC Store Builders.
Purchase a gift certificate to be used at Café Gratitude
KC for $1,000, and you will get a $1,200 gift certificate!
That's a 20 percent return on investment and will totally
support the opening of Café Gratitude!
    2. Attend one of our upcoming events: Community
Building Workshop, Abounding River Practice, or
intenSati.
    3. Ask yourself, friends, and family, "What are you
grateful for?"
    4. Sign up for our mailing list and we'll keep you
posted on our progress, events, and future ways you can
contribute.

I attended the opening preview event and the line to get in
wrapped around a city block. Once I was inside, the place was
packed with people celebrating with organic beer and wine to
the music of the Makepeace Brothers Band, but more than
anything, they were celebrating their place in a community—and
by all accounts, that's going to make for one healthy business
venture.

Below are the foundational elements that you must use as filters
when adding the community mind-set to your business, products,
processes, and services.

## Build Trust Through Content Creation

No matter how much you advertise your business, trust is built much
faster when people can find you and convince themselves that there
is value in adding you and your content to their daily life.

This is yet another strong reason to view content creation as a foundational and daily part of building your marketing business. This is not a piece of the puzzle that can be done in your spare time.

The importance of building trust is so high that I believe every business should employ a writer, either part-time or full-time, in the role of content creation and story building.

## Free Must Be Better

Examples of "freemium" models and free content strategies abound, and while this makes the strategy an expectation, it also raises the bar in terms of quality expectations.

It's no longer enough to offer a free but crippled version of the real deal as a way to upsell. In a community-based model, the mindset must be one of creating a free version so good that people will flock to get it, share it, and talk about it, and that a large percentage of those people will want to pay to get an even better version.

A commitment engine business must always ask, "How can we make what we give away better than what our competitors charge for?"

## Subscription Required

Today's hot community product is the subscription. Every business must look to build products, services, and experiences that create habitual consumption, participation, and perhaps more important, generate fees.

In order to gain mind share and make your community offering more than a onetime or an occasional purchase, consider a model that offers an experience that includes training, teaching, and sharing with other members of the community no matter what industry or product.

## Membership Rewards

The strongest community models, online and off, systemically reward the most active members of the community and use this reward system as a tool to create both social engagement and desire inside and outside of the community.

Private betas, complete with members-only invites, are a proven way to keep existing members engaged and to draw new members who want to do what it takes to get to the next level.

One has to look no further than the credit-card and airline industries to witness the power of the member rewards program. How can you tap the best of these kinds of programs to add to your community offerings?

One of the most overlooked member models is the co-op. While this may be slightly different from my suggestion of shared ownership, you can take ideas from this model and form community co-ops or purchasing co-ops that allow your customers to do things in groups that create benefits such as lower pricing and early access.

### Promote from Within

An essential element of your community-building platform is the consistent inclusion of community members in marketing campaigns.

Existing members should be incentivized to bring a friend to a workshop at no cost, get a special deal, benefit by sharing with their networks, or qualify for a high-quality perk in return for referring others to the community. This must be built into any launch or campaign.

Community is not something you build by simply installing a forum. To take advantage of the inherent benefits that this strategy offers, you must begin to talk internally and externally about your business as a network instead of as a sales organization.

## The Ultimate Measure of Marketing Success

For most businesses, the primary measures of marketing success are increased sales, better profits, and greater brand recognition.

That seems like a pretty obvious, logical, and healthy way to view marketing, doesn't it?

What if, however, the real goal was to build a trusting community? What if marketing decisions were made with the best interest of the customer community as the top priority? What if the ultimate measure of marketing success was a committed customer?

Know this: while your customers may love your products, may love doing business with you, and may adore the people you send to take care of them, what they ultimately determine is what all of this love does for them.

If this is true, and if your ultimate objective is to create customers who are totally committed to your business, you'll have to learn to view all of your decisions with the best interest of your customer in mind rather than the best interest of your business.

The distinction in this last statement may be subtle for some.

The difference, however, will show up when you start to question everything you do in this vein—will this decision benefit the community or will it simply benefit the business?

This questioning will prove harder than you think, because sometimes the answer might be "This will cost us a bundle, but it's the right thing to do."

You may have to learn how to tell your prospects and customers that they shouldn't buy a particular product or service because you know it's not right for them.

You may have to teach your customers how to get more from your products rather than buying more of them. You may have to teach them how to conserve rather than use up what you sell.

You may have to create and facilitate a customer community that can freely resell and trade what you sell.

Patagonia, a well-respected outdoor apparel and gear brand, recently created a platform in conjunction with eBay that makes it very easy for customers to resell and purchase used Patagonia gear.

Patagonia benefits very little directly from this move, but it has created something that I believe is very much in the best interest of its community.

Now, some of you might conclude that this is just a natural extension of the Patagonia brand of recycling and that all it's really done is aggregate a market that existed in places like Craigslist, until you dig into the companion initiative called the Common Threads Initiative.

This is the message Patagonia is using to build a committed customer, and it could come off as heresy to most hard-core marketers:

"Reduce. Don't buy what we don't need. Repair: Fix stuff that still has life in it. Reuse: Share. Then, only when you've exhausted those options, recycle."

In fact, they are asking customers to sign this pledge: "I agree to buy only what I need (and will last), repair what breaks, reuse (share) what I no longer need and recycle everything else."

While this initiative might actually cost Patagonia sales, it's the right message for the brand, it's the right message for the planet, and it may be the right message for the customer in the long run.

Making business decisions that benefit your customers first will almost always pay long-term dividends no matter how tough they may be from a short-term profit standpoint.

Telling a customer that your solution probably isn't the best and then ushering them to another, better solution, even one from a competitor, is the right thing to do and over time will create a totally loyal and committed customer willing to tell the world they can trust you.

## Building a Committed Community

Building a committed community begins with communicating a clear message that attracts community members.

Start by communicating your purpose to an external audience, putting your core beliefs on display in every product, service, and process, creating a customer experience that is filled with personality, and ultimately viewing your business as a place where an entire community can come to get more of what serves their purpose.

Every industry group feels that their business, their needs, their way of marketing is unique—that they are the only ones who must rely on word of mouth or referrals. While every industry has a unique set of clients, a unique language, maybe even an unusual distribution model, the way that customers come to know, like, and trust and form commitment is fundamentally the same.

What follows is the introduction to a core set of practices that every business can use to bring their passion and purpose to the building of a community. Each practice is so vital that I've also dedicated an entire chapter to the full explanation of how and why to bring them to life.

**Build and tell stories.** You must develop a set of core stories that you use in your business building. The stories help people understand how your business is different, not because of what it does so much, but because of what it cares about or doesn't do.

These stories must radiate from you, your staff, and your community and will ultimately make up the foundation of your brand promise.

**Reverse the experience.** The greatest way to deliver a remarkable marketing strategy is to deliver a remarkable marketing experience before, during, and after a customer is a customer.

In my previous book *The Referral Engine,* I shared my concept of the Marketing Hourglass. This concept has changed how tens of thousands of small-business owners view marketing as a whole.

Since publishing this tool, I've discovered how to use it to the fullest extent.

To borrow from a well-worn bit of wisdom, if you want to deliver an exceptional experience, you must start with the end in mind. You must begin the entire process by considering what you will do 90 or 180 days after you make a sale and then work backward to the point where you and the customer first meet.

**Sell by teaching.** You must commit to using education as your primary means of influence. This is one of the most powerful ways to differentiate your business in the eyes of those who come to work for you as well as those who come to experience your unique point of view.

When you embrace teaching in everything you do, your staff begins to understand that the company is their first customer.

**Become a platform.** It's no longer enough to think in terms of building a product or service. In fact, it's no longer enough to simply build a community of prospects, users, and buyers.

In order to truly differentiate, you must begin to think of your business as a platform for others to get what they need. You must expand your thinking from business to marketplace.

Can you create opportunity for strategic partners? Can you teach others how to launch businesses from your business? Can you mentor employees and become a hub for their personal growth?

These are questions that will take you far beyond the typical business-building mind-set, but the answers may become the higher purpose for your business.

To some, these ideas may feel foreign and not at all like a substantial way of doing business, but to others, they will ring true and real and perhaps for the first time they will be able to differentiate their business with perfect clarity.

**Install a community manager.** It's time for every business, regardless of size, to take note and add the role of community manager to its organization. Not because it's the hot trendy thing to do, but because it will change the way you think about growing your business.

If you think about the role of the community manager in the fullest sense, you'll come to understand the potential of having someone on staff who focuses specifically on the community aspects of your business.

Some limit their notion of the community manager to mean the person who responds to complaints on Twitter. What I want to propose is a much more comprehensive role.

Think of this person as playing the role of community host. Their job is to make sure that all of the community members feel appreciated, informed, and looked after.

The marketing team would still craft the messages to make this happen, sales would still create and nurture customer relationships, advertising would still generate leads, and customer service would still provide key follow-up and troubleshooting.

But the community manager would be running through it all as the person who makes sure the community as a whole is happy, healthy, and growing. That's the part many of us are missing and that's the part that can transform a business from satisfactory to remarkable.

The community manager is the one person in the organization who is focused on moving people logically through the steps of know, like, trust, try, buy, repeat, and refer, while also ensuring that all the members of your business ecosystem co-evolve their capabilities and roles and align themselves with the direction your organization is taking.

The community manager would in effect be an advocate for the members of your community and act to hold every department in the organization accountable for creating a better community experience.

There's nothing trendy or touchy-feely about this role; it's one of the most highly practical things any business can do right now and it's perhaps the only way to effectively merge the online and offline worlds in your business.

A community manager in today's world of business would:

- Look at what gets someone to sign up for your free e-book
- Obsess over the follow-up with potential community members
- Look for ways to help the organization know more about customers
- Manage Google+, Facebook, and Twitter communities
- Design ways to bring customers together
- Create and facilitate a formal strategic partner network
- Nudge the CEO to write more handwritten thank-you notes
- Build relationships with key industry and community journalists

- Participate in creating, maintaining, and curating the entire content grid
- Create a database of customer and prospect inquiries
- Look for ways to improve key customer touch points
- Work with clients to review and document results

You could add many more items to this list, but hopefully you're starting to see how this position might make a difference in your business. You could also argue that most of the items on this list should already be handled by sales or marketing or customer service.

The reality is that they're probably not being handled by anyone, and if they are, they are being handled without collaboration. One of the fundamental differences a community manager would provide is an entirely different view of the total organization. A view that crosses all departments and questions every contact and touch point as a conscientious host might do.

But mostly, this function acknowledges the fact that in today's world a thriving community is your greatest asset. It's time to make its care a central focus of your business.

# 18

# Sharing on Purpose

 **If there's a single thread** that I've tried to weave throughout this exploration of tapping passion, creating purpose, demonstrating a proposition, and displaying personality, it's that of sharing stories.

While we have spent a great deal of time so far talking about developing your internal stories and those that you use to lead your team, we now need to turn our attention to the story building that you use publicly as a vehicle for attracting like-minded community members and customers.

## Everyone Tells Stories

It's important to realize that every successful company is already using its marketing muscles to tell stories. The question is, are they the right stories, are they the authentic stories, and are they the stories that tell the mission from the inside out?

And there's another story to consider. The story our customers tell themselves about the products, services, and brands they choose to make connections with.

When we fail to communicate our purpose and reason for

existing in our marketing, we run the risk of losing our most power-ful story. When we try to craft stories or value propositions that we think our prospects want to hear, we give up control of the real story and in effect force our customers to create their own version of the story.

This is how brands end up with very muddled identities.

The trick is to find the essence of your stories and work with your customers to make them a part of it. Your story about overcoming obstacles in your past might make a great story when told at an event or company meeting, but unless your customers and prospects understand how the story relates to their situation, objectives, and needs, it will never take on the life that it needs to become a com-munity asset.

You must find a way to make your story of passion and purpose interesting to the audience you want to influence. The best way to do this is to find a way to make the listener feel interesting too.

## Who's the Hero Now?

As you may recall, very early on in this work I asked you to consider who you needed to see you as a hero. This line of thinking is meant to help you form a picture of those you aim to serve as a central theme of working on purpose.

At this point in the journey, I want you to flip the thinking around a bit and ask this question:

## How Do You Make Your Customers the Hero of Your Story?

I use the idea of the hero a fair amount when I talk about building a business. I don't use it in an egotistic way, more as a kind of ideal. I think aspiring to be a hero to someone is a good thing.

You can substitute *leader* if you like, but I love the image of hero because I think it paints a much more vivid illustration of the whole package—struggle, denial, acceptance, achievement, and purpose.

While I think it's important that you and your business strive to be the hero in somebody's story, I think it's equally important that you understand how to position your customer or community as the hero of your story.

**Learn their backstory.** Before you can really thrust your customers into the hero's role, you have to know who they are, and you find that out by knowing where they came from, what's bugging them, and what they really would rather have that they don't have.

This kind of information isn't rentable; you have to dig; and this starts with asking, listening, and paying close attention. I don't know how you might manage this, but I've always thought the greatest marketing research tool you could ever create is a family dinner. You could learn more than you would ever need to know about a person by going with them to their parents' house for dinner one Sunday.

So, short of that, how could you learn what makes them tick? Spend time and earn the right to learn about them outside of your business context. Follow everything they share in social media; it's a lot like Sunday dinner in there at times.

There is no greater way to earn trust than to demonstrate that you know their story.

**Give them an antagonist.** Every great story has a bad guy or girl; it's what makes us cheer for the good guy or girl.

There are times when you draw your customer closer by simply helping them understand who or what the antagonist is. Sometimes they don't even realize what the problem is that your business can solve. Many times you have to help them see the extent of the enemy's grip.

Now, more often than not the word *antagonist* here is simply a metaphor for a challenge like leaking profit, poor time management, wasted effort, lost opportunity, living in pain, or needless risk, but you have to help them understand what they are up against.

**Call them to duty.** In order for someone to be a hero, they must be called—they must have an idea to serve.

Your marketing story must give them hope that they have the

power to overcome whatever the challenge is. I know this sounds a little dramatic, but that's the point; a connection to a higher purpose or at least a meaningful idea is much stronger than simply trying to convince someone that they need what you have to offer.

In order to create impact in the life of your customers, they need to feel like what you have to offer is hope and empowerment. Those are pretty strong words and you've got to believe them if your customer is going to be the center of your story.

**Help them persevere.** Once you've demonstrated that you know who your customer is, you know what a rough time she's endured trying to get results, and you know what overcoming her challenges might look like for her, you've got to be prepared to demonstrate that you'll be there with her until she does overcome.

I guess you could demonstrate this most easily in your sales, service, and follow-up, but it must be a part of the story that your customer understands is a given.

**Free them.** Finally, help them understand the results they've achieved, help them measure just how far they've come, how much impact they're making on your business and perhaps in the lives of those they now impact.

Since I'm attempting to apply these rather abstract ideas to no particular business, I know some will find this idea a bit confusing.

Here's my suggestion: grab a piece of marketing copy you currently share with customers and ask yourself this series of questions:

- Does it demonstrate that we get who they are?
- Does it paint a picture of the real challenges they face?
- Does it provide hope for what a future without those challenges could be like?
- Does it give a solution for how those challenges could be addressed?
- Does it offer proof that others are indeed experiencing these results?

How can you let them see that they are the ones who must experience the changes required to make a difference?

How can you get them to echo your story and make it their story?

Understanding the persona of your ideal client is the first step in creating a marketing strategy that will allow you to effectively carve out a market to build the kind of momentum you need. When you view your market as a personality, you can begin to speak to each customer in a language that builds trust on the most personal level. But first you must know their story!

**Question your demographic.** Look at your current customers. What are the characteristics shared by your most profitable, referral-generating customers? Understand and catalog what you can as a starting point for getting a clearer picture of your demographic.

**Narrow your sights.** Once you start to get a better view of your profitable customers, it's time to take a good, hard look at the other 70 percent. You know, the ones you took on because you couldn't say no or because it had been a slow month or because you'd done some business with them for years. Every organization has those customers and I'm suggesting you purge (some of) them. In order for you to shape your ideal customer strategy, you need a very clear picture of the clients you don't want and you need to start saying no.

**Social media adds focus.** Collecting psychographic and behavioral data on a market is a common practice for marketers, as it adds much richer information than statistical data can provide. Collecting this kind of information used to be expensive and less than personal. Social media adoption has altered this piece of the puzzle in interesting ways. People joke about people talking about what they had for dinner on Twitter, but that kind of information, while seemingly inane, is marketing gold. Append your entire customer list with everything you can know through social media and you will discover more about what motivates and drives your customers than years of research could ever reveal—including which ones wield influence and love to connect and refer.

**Visualize real people.** Once you've done the research above on your ideal client, it's time to start getting visual. Write out a description of a real ideal client whom you would love ten more of. Write everything you can think of: what they look like, what they think, what they want, what they fear, what they think fun, risk, and passion look like. Use photos of real people to help you create this total persona and then hang it on the wall for all your employees to absorb. Maybe you need to do this a couple of times and develop several distinct ideal client personality types, but imagine if you put these images and descriptions on the wall and referred to them as you made sales calls, wrote Web copy, or brainstormed about a product innovation. It's like having the customers in the meeting with you. In fact, go a bit over the top and create life-size ideal client cutouts and invite Bill and Mary and Tom into your meetings. At the very least, it will add some fun to the meeting.

## What If You Don't Have a Customer Database to Draw Research From?

**1. Start with the smallest market possible.** This may feel counterintuitive to many who are just starting a business, but you have to find a group of customers who think what you have to offer is special. When you're just getting started, you may have very little to offer and in many cases very few resources with which to make sufficient noise in a market for generic solutions.

Your key is to find a very narrow group, with very specific demographics or a very specific problem or need, and create raving fans out of this group. You can always expand your reach after you gain traction, but you can also become a big player in this smaller market as you grow.

**2. Create an initial value hypothesis.** In the step above, I mentioned the idea of finding a narrow group that finds what you have to offer special. Of course, this implies that you do indeed have something to offer that is special.

You must create a "why us" value proposition and use that as your hypothesis for why us. If this is starting to sound a little like science, that's because it is. You must always stay in test and refine mode in order to move forward.

Many people get caught up in trying to execute their business plan when the fact of the matter is the market doesn't care about your business plan. The only thing that matters is what you discover and apply out there in the lab beyond your office.

**3. Get real in discovery test sessions.** Established, thriving businesses have the ability to learn a great deal every day from customer interaction. Since start-ups don't have any customer interaction, they have to create ways to test their theories initially and on the fly.

The key to both making and affirming your initial assumptions is to set up what I call discovery test sessions with prospects who might easily fit into your initial smallest market group. These are essentially staged one-on-one meetings.

This can be a little tricky since you have no relationship with said prospect. I often find that there are industry or trade groups that may contain your initial target market, and by joining these, you may have an easier time gaining access to this group.

Another possible option is to offer free sample products or beta-test relationships to those willing to provide you with agreed-upon feedback.

The main thing is that you start talking to prospects about what they need, what they think, what works, what doesn't, and what they don't have now. This is how you evolve your business, your features, and your assumptions based on serving a narrowly defined target.

**4. Draw an ideal customer sketch.** Once you've trotted out your hypothesis and tested it with your narrow group, you've got to go to work on discovering and defining everything you can about your ideal target group.

Some of this information, such as demographics, will be widely understood, but much of it will be discovered in your test sessions and through some additional research in more behavior-oriented places such as social media.

This is a great time to start your CRM thinking by building custom customer profiles that include much richer information than most people capture.

**5. Add strategy model components.** The final step is to apply this new ideal customer approach to other elements of your strategy.

The thing is, when you discover your initial ideal client, it should impact the thinking about your basic business model and overall business strategy. All great business models are customer-focused, and now that you have a picture of this customer, it's time to consider how this alters the other aspects of your business.

Consider now how this discovery might impact your offerings, your revenue streams, distribution channels, and even pricing.

Consider how you can reach this market, who you can partner with, and what resources you either have or need to have in order to make an impact in this market.

I can tell you that my experience suggests that you're never really done with this exercise. As your business evolves, as you learn and grow, this model will evolve as well, but perhaps the continual process of discovery is just as important as what you discover.

## A Database for Your Customer

Once you start to get a feel for accessing this kind of personal information, you can begin to change your concept of the client database. Instead of looking at it as a tool for you, flip it and make it a tool for them. In other words, start building a database that contains everything you can know about your customers and use it to make them feel special. Use it to note when significant things have happened, listen to what they are saying in social media, and engage on a personal level, send them a birthday gift, or remind them that it's their anniversary. Every once in a while sit down with them and ask them to share. It might start with them sharing something about your products and services, but ultimately, if you take this practice to heart, the conversation will turn to them sharing how you can help them achieve their goals.

## Listening for Backstories

The best way to bring the listener's fears, hopes, dreams, and goals into your stories is to get very, very good at listening to your customers' backstories.

A backstory is used to help fill in the details about a character so that readers have a better understanding of the character's motives and decisions. Many times authors will reveal the backstory in bits and pieces to create additional drama or anticipation for upcoming plot twists.

Marketers can use this same device when it comes to better understanding what really makes their customers tick and what really inspires and excites them to action and commitment.

Your backstory research should include filling in the details for some hard-to-access information such as:

- What brings our customers joy?
- What are they worried about?
- What challenges do they face?
- What do they hope to gain from us?
- What goals are they striving to attain?
- What experience thrills them?
- Where do they get their information?
- Whom do they trust most?

## The Core Questions You Must Ask Every Customer

Constantly seeking feedback from your customers is a great way to learn how to market your business more effectively. If you've never done this before, begin to do it immediately, as it is one of the best ways to discover how to integrate your internal stories in ways that make them relevant to your most important community members.

I can't tell you how many times I've worked with a small business that had no idea why customers were so committed until they heard it right from the mouths of some happy customers. Seeking feedback is also a great way to get better and plug gaps.

Below are five questions I like to pose to customers, as they can provide a great discussion base for getting at what's truly important to you and your customers. Create a form and get into the habit of surveying a handful of customers every month. I think you'll be rewarded with tremendous insight and you'll also find that your customers enjoy being asked what they think.

One word of caution; don't accept vague answers like "You provide good service." While that may be true and good to hear, you can't work with it. Push a bit and ask what good service looks like and maybe even if they can tell you a backstory about a specific instance in which they felt they got good service.

### 1. What made you decide to hire us/buy from us in the first place?

This is a good baseline question for your marketing. It can get at how well your advertising, message, and lead conversion processes are working. I've also heard customers talk about the personal connection or culture that felt right in this question.

### 2. What's one thing we do better than others you do business with? Or, what's the one thing you love most about what we do for you?

In this question you are trying to discover something that you can work with as a true differentiator. This is probably the question you'll need to work hardest at getting a specific answer to. You want to look for words and phrases and actual experiences that keep coming up over and over again, no matter how insignificant they may seem to you. As your customers are explaining in their own words what you do best, they are likely providing clues as to how to connect your story with their story.

### 3. What's one thing you don't have from any other source that you wish you could find?

On the surface this question could be looked at as a customer service improvement question, and it may be, but the true gold in this question is found when your customers are able to identify an innovation. Sometimes we go along doing what we've always done and then out of the blue a customer says something like "I sure wish it came like this," and all of a sudden it's painfully clear how you can create a meaningful innovation to your products, services, and processes. Push your customers to describe the perfect experience of buying what you sell.

### 4. Do you refer us to others, and if so, what words do you use?

This is the ultimate question about satisfaction because a truthful answer means your customer likes the product and likes the experience of getting the product. (You can substitute *service* here of course.) There's an entire consulting industry cropping up around helping people discover what Fred Reichheld called the Net Promoter Score in his book *The Ultimate Question*.

Small businesses can take this a step further and start understanding specifically why they get referrals and perhaps the exact words and phrases a customer might use when describing to a friend why their company is the best.

It is next to impossible to leave their story out of this formula.

### 5. What would you Google to find a business like ours?

This is the new lead generation question, but understanding what it implies is very important. If you want to get very, very good at being found online, around the world, or around the town, you have to know everything you can about the actual terms and phrases your customers use when they go looking for companies like yours.

Far too often businesses optimize their Web sites around industry jargon and technical terms when what people are really searching for is "stuff to make my life better."

## Presenting Stories

In most businesses, there will be times when presenting your stories moves beyond words on a page or an online profile.

Presenting your story to potential investors, customers, and partners live and in person (or via online video) is one of the most powerful ways to help your audience both understand and feel your passion and purpose.

As a business grows, this can become the most important task of the leader and it's a skill that must be learned and practiced.

If you want to up your presentation skills or teach someoné in your organization to present your core stories visually, you should pick up Nancy Duarte's books, *Resonate: Present Visual Stories That Transform Audiences* and *slide:ology: The Art and Science of Creating Great Presentations,* or any of the works in the Presentation Zen series by Garr Reynolds.

You might also consider seeking out a storytelling festival in your community or contacting the International Storytelling Center or the Center for Digital Storytelling.

## Staff as Storyteller

With so much emphasis placed on the art of story building and storytelling, it should come as no surprise that a great deal of your staff development should center around helping them understand how to both connect their own personal backstories to the values of the organization and find ways to consistently communicate those stories in the appropriate settings.

Two examples I shared earlier in this book serve as great illustrations.

When I interviewed a handful of staff members at the Chicago-based T-shirt printer Threadless, I was struck by their personal stories of being members of the community first and then doing whatever it took to come on board. Many members of the marketing team had started their careers at Threadless working in the warehouse and moved into positions that allowed them to interact and tell their stories more directly to and through the community in places like the company's Facebook page.

The amount of YouTube video storytelling that goes on by staff members of Appletree Answers is a testament to the power of sharing on purpose that can happen throughout an organization.

This is an easy way for newly acquired community partners as well as new hires and new customers to develop a great sense of the depth of culture, teamwork, and spirit that goes on internally in a company, and they will be drawn to the stories of personal passion and achievement.

# 19

# Reverse Engineer Everything

**As I've stated before in** this book, marketing is essentially getting someone who has a need to know, like, and trust you to purchase your product. Of course, once you have accomplished this, you must turn that **know, like,** and **trust** into **try, buy, repeat,** and **refer.**

That is the entire practice of marketing summed up in seven little words that make up what I call the Marketing Hourglass.

The idea behind the hourglass is that you look at each of the seven stages and intentionally plan products, services, processes, and points of contact that logically move prospects along to the point where they become customers and then receive such a remarkable customer experience they become repeat customers and referral advocates. I talk a great deal about building your hourglass in *The Referral Engine.*

If you do nothing but spend the time filling in the blanks in each of the stages listed below, you will be miles ahead in your thinking about a simple yet powerful approach to your marketing.

The key is to systematically develop touch points, processes, and product/service offerings for each of the seven phases of the hourglass.

1. Know—ads, article, and referred leads
2. Like—Web site, reception, and e-mail newsletter
3. Trust—marketing kit, white papers, and sales presentations
4. Try—Webinars, evaluations, and nurturing activities
5. Buy—fulfillment, new customer kit, delivery, and financial arrangements
6. Repeat—post-customer survey, cross-sell presentations, and quarterly events
7. Refer—results reviews, partner introductions, peer-to-peer Webinars, and community building

## Turn Things Around

When most businesses create a new product or service offering, they initially develop the attributes of the product or service. This makes sense since you don't have anything to sell unless you create something people want to buy.

But the very next thing they do, once they think they have a winner on their hands, is to go to work on the promotion of the new offering—the sales letter, landing page, brochure.

Again, another important marketing consideration, but I would like to suggest a much stronger path.

## Begin with the End in Mind

The very first thing you should do when thinking about bringing a product or service to market is to think about what you want customers to be thinking and feeling about your product or service 180 days or so after they made the purchase and work backward toward the point where they become interested in making a purchase.

The processes, contacts, and follow-ups you build by taking this "customer experience" approach can help ensure that you have a winner, promote a winner, and perhaps more important thrill your customer.

In the rush to create and promote our goods, it's this final, crucial point that often goes without thought or is made up after a repeat sales and referrals lag.

Think of it this way: the sale is not complete until the customer is so happy that she confidently makes referrals.

An example of looking at the process backward for a training course you're promoting might look something like this:

- **180 days after purchase.** Customer receives free course updates and offers to meet with a select group of other course participants in an invitation-only peer-to-peer group accountability program.
- **90 days after purchase.** Customer receives e-mail offering them 30 percent off on any other product or service of their choice as a current customer courtesy.
- **60 days after purchase.** Customer receives coupon offering free evaluation of their progress with the training course and the opportunity to engage a consultant to help them if they are stuck working on their own.
- **30 days after purchase.** Customer receives coupon for free sixty-minute coaching session to help keep them on track.
- **14 days after purchase.** Customer receives coupon for thirty days of unlimited e-mail support to keep them on track with their purchase.
- **7 days after purchase.** Customer receives mailing with additional bonus materials as a way of saying thank you for their purchase.
- **Immediately on purchase.** On successful shopping-cart transaction, customer is directed to a Web page that hosts a welcome video that sets the expectation for when and how they will receive their purchase. Automated e-mail provides

instructions and orients the customer to the contents of their new purchase and how to ask for support if they have questions.

- **Trial.** After viewing a video series, the prospect is offered the opportunity to download two free chapters from the course and receive a free thirty-minute coaching session to discuss their specific challenges.
- **Information gathering.** After the seminar prospect is offered an opportunity to sign up to receive the video series of client case studies and e-book featuring content covered in the seminar.
- **Awareness.** The first step calls for a prospect to attend an informational online seminar that dives into the problems most businesses in their industry face when trying to do X.

Obviously, the components of this approach will vary greatly depending upon the offering and prospective customer, but it's the thinking here that's important.

The process of beginning with the end in mind actually forces improvement on the product or service, creates opportunities to upsell and cross-sell, and focuses on the long-term positive experience for the customer, which creates lead generation by way of referral and word of mouth.

One final word of advice: Don't make this a stiff, automated, spammy drip system. Put personality, fun, surprise, and value into each and every contact.

## Gain Small Commitments

The ultimate dream of any marketer is to go from "Hi, how are you?" to "And what form of payment will you be using today?" in sixty seconds or less.

The process, and yes, it is a process, of gaining enough know, like, and trust to make a sale is a thoughtful one. It certainly can happen by putting enough good stuff out into the world and having all of that come together in the happy accident that is a customer, but there's a psychology that can be employed to make it happen in a more predictable manner as well.

The key is to engage your prospects in a series of small movements. You may not be able to go from awareness to purchase, but you may be able to move from "Okay, tell me more" to "Hmm, this looks interesting," and then to the even more exciting "I think you really get my problem."

By creating a systematic path that asks your prospects to make tiny commitments, you can involve them in a story of their own making and eventually earn the right to sell them your value-laden products and services.

The following criteria should be considered as you design your process to get little commitments.

## Gain Involvement

The first step is to engage the prospect in process. One of the best ways to engage anyone is to ask a question with a personal interest. For example: "Which best describes you? Are you more of an X or more of a Y?"

You can pose this question in a simple pop-up form on your Web site, and just by doing so, you create a tiny commitment in the prospects that provide this information.

## Personalized Branching

The second step in the process is to tailor information based on responses. Something we all crave is information that we believe is specifically tailored to our situation or need. And the fact is, scientific research has shown that we are much more likely to trust and therefore believe information that we perceive as personalized.

Creating branching paths of information that allow people to personalize what they receive from you is a very powerful way to build trust. Many form tools, such as Wufoo, allow you to ask question one and then determine question two based on the answer to question one. So if question one is "Are you interested in information about sailing or fishing?" question two will be very different for those who answer "fishing" than for those who answer "sailing."

Your survey tool can also then redirect your prospect to a specific sign-up page that delivers a specific autoresponder series, based solely on their responses.

## Help Them Trust Their Decisions

The final piece of this puzzle is the delivery of information tailored to the stated needs of the individual. Now, you can take this as far as you want or as false as you want. Studies have shown that people are much more likely to trust information that they perceive is tailored to their specific answers even if it's actually generic. There's something in us that wants to believe the information is true because we participated in its creation. (Think horoscopes.)

I'm not suggesting that you lead people down a path that promises a custom solution and then deliver the same information to everyone, but I am stating this to demonstrate the power of tiny commitments. If someone has participated in a series of tiny commitments, they are much more likely to want to believe they are now getting the perfect information for their unique situation, so help them trust this decision by giving it to them.

The way to get the most from this idea is to truly develop personalized sets of questions and complementary sets of tailored information to move people to the point where their next commitment involves their wallet.

# The Stages of the New Sales Cycle

Generating and converting leads is mostly what marketing is about. Creating happy customers is mostly what generates long-term profit.

In this pursuit, marketers have long realized that there is a definite cycle that must occur in most businesses in order to get a prospect's interest and then turn that interest into dollars.

Many businesses have differing cycles depending upon the complexity or cost of the purchase being considered. Some have cycles that are triggered by events, such as the birth of a child or start of a business.

The sales cycle, like most every other aspect of marketing, has been impacted dramatically by the Internet, the content and information glut, and a prospect's ability to block uninvited messages.

Today's sales cycle contains distinct segments and smart marketers understand they must build new touch points, content, and processes to address the logical progression of prospect into raving fan in order to compete in today's world.

Below are the five stages in the new sales cycle.

**Listen.** The very first stage of the sales cycle today involves intent listening. Prospects today serve up a buffet of information via social media and we can gain incredible access to their challenges, requests, chain of command, and recent changes—basically a selling road map—if we only listen.

**Shine.** Nobody talks about boring businesses. To create awareness these days, you must communicate a clear difference, create content people readily choose to share, and actively participate in dozens of outposts frequented by your ideal prospects. Getting noticed these days is less about shouting and more about sparkling.

**Educate.** Once awareness is created, we must build trust for our products, services, solutions, and expertise. Content, both written and spoken, is what sells.

**Convert.** Lead conversion, or what most small businesses still refer to as selling, is a profoundly changed activity in this model. If the sales cycle has been followed to this point, there is very little selling that remains to be done. The job here is to make sure the prospect can see how he can get the desired results with your solution. This is still an education and content play, but now it's all about showing proof and forecasting results in your system or process.

**Repeat.** The final stage of the sales process is a return to listening, but now we are listening to a customer. We are listening for what works, what doesn't, how to get better results, how to measure results, how to engage them further, and how to turn a thrilled customer into a highly active referral source.

A happy customer is the most powerful lead generation tool in the new marketer's tool chest and creates the kind of business-building momentum that makes this a pretty simple game.

## Keeping a Community Member Happy Is the New Form of Lead Generation

Used to be that we could go out there and hunt down new leads and customers with measured precision. We found a message that worked, found a medium that reached the right folks, tested, measured, refined, and bingo—turn on the tap to growth.

And then a couple of things happened. Our prospects developed tools wise enough to block and ignore messages, social media platforms turned the equation into a dialogue rather than a monologue, and the worst recession in years crippled our prospects' confidence.

Customer loss, something that might have been acceptable at some point in your trajectory, is devastating in today's market reality.

Today, a lost customer costs a business in two very significant ways.

First, replacing a customer has become harder to do, and perhaps more important, a happy customer is the greatest lead generation tool available. A thrilled customer is the most potent marketing asset your organization can leverage. Smart marketers realize this and explore ways to collaborate, enable, and grow with their existing customers as a powerful lead generation channel.

Keeping a customer happy doesn't stop at delivering on your promise. While not every company even passes that test, there is an expectation that you will deliver. To turn your customers into collaborative partners, you've got to up your total customer experience game.

I know everyone talks about this, but what does it really mean in the practical everyday world?

It's more than just creating a fun and exciting experience. I think those are important, but turning your customers into committed partners requires an experience that possesses mutually beneficial elements. Customers must get something in return for their commitment.

Below are some of the elements I think you need to consider in an effort to draw your customers close enough to turn them into committed partners.

## Personalize the Follow-up

You need to stay top of mind and you need to keep in touch, but that's a minimum-level effort. If you want to stand out, you need to personalize your follow-up by connecting with your customers via social networks and exploring ways to tailor your message to their world. You need to ask them frequently about what they need to know, hear, read, and consume, and find ways to deliver that.

## Review Results

Your marketing and customer service processes must contain a way for you to help your customers realize the impact of working with you. You must gauge this for your own sake and so that you can find and fix occasions when something didn't work as planned. Imagine how much business leaks from organizations because clients don't have the time, energy, or desire to find out how to get what they thought they were going to get. If you don't do this step, you're throwing money away.

### Publish Together

Every one of our customers has a suite of publishing tools available to him. They can blog about us, create video product demos, review us, and tweet sweet little nothings with very little effort or cost. Oh, and the search engines really kind of love to find all that stuff too.

So, if you want to draw your customers in deeper, get in the publishing game with them. Teach them how to use these tools and then find ways to shoot success stories together, let them guest blog post and respond to comments, show them how to write reviews and find other great resources on review sites. Most importantly, find a way to show them why doing this is good for them.

### Pair with Peers

One of the greatest gifts you can give your customers is to facilitate their networking efforts. In most cases, some segment of your market consists of customers who are peers in some way—all small-business CEOs, all purchasing agents, etc.

What if you found ways to create roundtable discussion communities and brought these peers together to discuss meaningful developments in their industry? What if some of these were customers and some were not? Do you see how you, your customers, and your lead generation efforts could benefit from this?

### Be Sharable

One of the easiest ways to empower your thrilled customers is to make your content as sharable as possible.

Add sharing plugins, "like" and "retweet" buttons, and make it very easy to pass your e-books, slides, and e-mail newsletters.

### Gather

A couple of times a year, take small groups of your customers to lunch. You don't have to do much more than bring them together and let them meet. You will be surprised how often they find ways they can help one another.

Once in a while bring as many of your customers together as you can. Acknowledge your referral champions and create a video booth where they can share their testimonials and success stories.

# 20

# Teaching as Selling

 **Throughout this book, I've talked** about the idea of turning your business into a place where people can connect and feel alive.

Many of the tactics used for building a strong culture are founded on the principles of teaching. Employees learn to self-manage when they are taught autonomy and shown transparency.

When this is how the company operates internally, it's quite natural for employees to transfer this form of teaching to the act of community building and even selling. When purpose and passion are communicated as the primary value proposition, then the content needed to attract and convert prospects is the telling of the story that represents the higher purpose in a logical and consistent fashion.

There is an authentic path that your community-building content must follow, and it almost resembles a curriculum that you might encounter in doing course work. The goal is to move prospects through a funnel-like fashion toward taking tiny steps and making small commitments to move to the next level of content. There are logical content prerequisites that a community member must consume and there are advanced forms of both learning and teaching that eventually build the level of commitment required to make a purchase and refer a friend.

The ultimate goal and test of commitment is when you can begin to involve your community in the teaching aspects of growing your business, including the act of building loyalty and enhancing the experience your entire community receives.

Robin Robins, founder of Marketing Technology Toolkit, involves her customer community in an incredible way. She has created a membership program that allows her mostly IT business customers to receive ongoing business-building support through coaching, training, and tools she provides.

She has created what she calls "accountability groups" in the membership program; customers head up these groups and do a great deal of work keeping participants engaged and on track. Heading up these groups is not a paid position, but is done by loyal and committed customers who want to play a bigger role in the community.

## The Five Types of Content Your Community Needs

The creation and distribution of content has become such a significant aspect of effective marketing and teaching that it requires a high place in the marketing strategy conversation in most every business.

Some might go as far as to suggest content marketing has become the most effective way to build a business or sell a product.

Strategically, the word *content* must mean more than a blog post or a blank sheet of paper each day. You must begin to think of your content as a total body of work that is being built to serve your business over time.

You must understand and create content for the most important key-word phrases for your industry, the essential themes of education in your business, your core beliefs, and your company's core points of differentiation.

You must also think in terms of your content as a tool that moves prospects from awareness to conversion and in this effort there are at least five types of content that you must address. Each type must be considered as part of your overall content strategy.

**Content that builds trust.** One of the first jobs of your content is to bridge the gap from awareness to trust building. Your SEO efforts actually marry with this type of content to make sure you are found often.

- "How to" content—specific advice or tips and tricks.
- Reviews—customer reviews on sites like Yelp and Google Places.
- Testimonials—endorsements from happy customers.
- Articles—articles you've written or that mention your firm in outside publications.

**Content that educates.** Once you create awareness and trust, a prospect will be hungry to find out much more about your unique approach, your solution, your story, and your organization.

- e-books—not boring, dry technical stuff, but your best writing tying together a bigger topic, perhaps a series of previously published blog posts.
- Newsletters—weekly or monthly education that nurtures a customer's interest.
- Seminars—in person or online, these allow prospects to learn as well as engage.
- FAQs—some folks just need the answers to their questions and this format serves well.
- Survey data—results from surveys can be very compelling as a way to let prospects know you understand them.

**Community-generated content.** Getting your customers involved in the production of content builds loyalty and community, creates proof of results, and gives you another avenue for content creation.

- Automatic referrals and reviews—create ways to move happy customers to a referral and review process.
- Testimonials—automate this process by providing online audio and video tools.
- Video success stories—create events that bring customers together to tell their story and network.

**Other people's content.** One of the primary jobs of marketers these days is to provide some insight into the stream of information that our customers face. Filtering and aggregating content produced by others is not only a great service, it's a great differentiator.

- Custom RSS feeds—create customer- or industry-specific feeds to share.
- Republish, Share, RT—point to and share great content that is being produced.
- Curate—use tools like Storify to collect and republish customer newsletters.

**Content that converts.** This last category is one that gets overlooked in the write for writing's sake view of content. Ultimately, great content has the ability to call and convert prospects to the action of buying.

- In-person events—live events are the absolute best way to use content to close.
- Case studies—deep studies into the success of another client act as tangible proof in the buying decision.
- ROI calculators—use content to help prospects understand the specific value of making a change.
- Results—provide documented-proof results in simple and easy-to-understand forms that address the common needs of most prospects.

## How to Get Your Community to Create Content

You've heard enough about the need to produce content that I'm guessing you're probably blogging away and curating, aggregating, and filtering all manner of content. But there's one type of content that you may not be focused on and I happen to think it's one of the most potent to be had—customer-generated content.

Your customers, the ones who already know, like, and trust you, are more equipped to tell the real story of your business than an army of writers in any marketing department, so why not engage them to do just that?

Imagine taking your best, most loyal, most vocal customer with you on your next sales call and asking her to simply explain the real benefits she's realized because of the work you've done for her. That's the power of customer-generated content when done right and that's why you need to routinely find ways to acquire it.

Below are five ideas to help you get your customers to start telling their stories.

### One-Question Testimonial

Create a survey that asks every customer one question with the customer able to rate your business on a scale of one to ten. Now set the survey up so that if the answer is one to four, the survey taker is redirected to a page that apologizes and sets the expectation that he will hear from someone immediately to find out what went wrong.

If it's a five to seven, send the customer to a page that says you're not happy until she is happier and ask her to suggest how you could have done better.

For the eight-to-ten answers, redirect them to a form that allows them to submit a testimonial and ask them to check a box if they would agree to be interviewed for a case study.

This is a great way to automate testimonial generation and keep a real-time pulse on how you're doing. I use Wufoo forms to run this process, but I've heard good things about Formstack as well.

## Video Appreciation Party

I've written about this before, but it's such a great way to get lots of great video content that I thought I would share it again.

Once a year or so, hold a client appreciation event to say thanks and create a networking event for your clients and prospects. Hire a video crew for the event, and after a few bottles of wine have been emptied, ask some of your clients to talk about their experience with your firm on camera. Then also let them record a five-minute commercial for their own use.

This is a great way to get lots of testimonials and case studies in one day and your clients will get very engaged in swapping stories and selling one another on the benefits of working with you.

## Tell Us Your Story

Getting your customers to share their experience is a very powerful form of content. You can sit across the desk and interview them in order to extract this kind of content or you can employ a handful of tools that make it very easy to capture these stories.

For audio-only content, a testimonial recording line from Audio-Acrobat is a great way to go. You simply provide your customers with a phone number that they can call and record their story. The service then produces an MP3 and code to embed on your site for people to play the recordings.

You can also use a tool like MailVU that allows you to send a link with a video capture tool so your clients with a webcam can record a video testimonial or story and submit it with little work on your part.

### Community Knowledge Base

What if you could find a way to get your best customers to willingly shoulder the responsibility of creating answers to questions and best practices? Tools like Zendesk and Get Satisfaction make it easy for you to enable community members to provide help and archived advice to other customers and prospects.

### Help Your Peers

Using a tool like Google+ Hangouts, Skype Video Conference, or GoToMeeting Video Conference, you can easily host and facilitate a group video conference where your customers and their peers can discuss important industry and business challenges and trends. You can record and archive the event and create some very useful and engaging content.

This is not a sales event, but by virtue of the fact that you have included customers in the conversation, there will be the inevitable discussions about what you've done to help them address a challenge.

Creating opportunities to capture the stories your clients have to tell is an important piece in any fully developed content strategy.

## How to Use Other People's Content

You need lots of content, you know that, but you also know that content creation is one of the more time-intensive marketing activities you have to tackle.

While you do need to create your own content as the foundation for your total content and teaching strategy, you can—and should—supplement your content with that from other people.

One of the best services marketers can provide these days is to act as a filter for all that's being produced out there and select the best of the best on behalf of their communities.

Finding and sharing consistently high-quality, relevant content and adding insight to this information not only is a great way to increase the volume of your content but is a great way to build trust in the value of your content.

Here are five ways to add other people's content to your routine.

## Cobrand a Winner

Lots of people produce great content in the form of downloadable white papers and e-books. In some cases they do this to attract newsletter subscribers and links, but quite often they do it because they know something about a topic and want to document it.

With just a little bit of searching, you can probably turn up a great e-book that your network would love to get their hands on. Now, some people might simply link to this content, but I'd like to suggest another way.

What if you approached the e-book author and asked if you could send it out to your networks, with full credit to the author, but with the ability to add one simple information page about you or your company at the back?

You could potentially build a library of content overnight with the right topics and content.

Here's how to get started.

Use the Google filetype operator to find lots of potential candidates on just about any topic you can imagine. Here's how it works. If you want to find PDF documents and e-books about content curation, for example, you would type: "content curation filetype:pdf" into a Google search box.

This tells Google you are looking for content related to content curation, but you only want results that are PDF files. This way you'll probably turn up any number of candidates for cobranding projects.

## E-mail Newsletter Snacks

Publishing a weekly e-mail newsletter is a proven way to stay top of mind with your community. Of course, offering a great free e-book as mentioned above is a great way to build that weekly news-letter list.

As you compete for in-box space, you must keep in mind that your newsletter content must be consistently useful, relevant, and convenient.

One of the best ways to meet these qualifications is to produce high-quality content filtered from other sources and delivered in snack-size bites. Think in terms of an e-mail newsletter that might contain five to six great articles presented with abstracts that lay out in about a hundred words what someone might want to click through and read the rest of.

Using tools like Alltop, Google Reader, Newsvine, or PopUrls, you can easily locate and aggregate content related to topics of interest to your readers. You may also be able to locate local bloggers who could be great candidates for guest content and strategic relationships.

## Curate a Magazine

The idea of curating content is very hot right now, but in order to really make it pay you've also got to be ready to add insight. So many people look at curation as something more closely aligned with republishing.

Republishing content you find does have value, but narrowly targeting a very specific topic and becoming known as a trusted source of insight on the vast array of information being published on any topic is how you take content curation to a new level.

Below are some of my favorite tools for creating your curated online content magazines.

- mySyndicaat—http://mysyndicaat.com/home
- Scoop.it—http://www.scoop.it
- Storify—http://storify.com
- Curation Station—http://curationstation.com

You can also use tools like Delicious, Evernote, Pinterest, or Pearltrees—http://www.pearltrees.com/—to simply clip, bookmark, and organize content you find for republication.

If you want to really know how to get great at this, follow the work of Robin Good and start by reading "What Makes a Great Curator Great?" at www.masternewmedia.org/what-makes-a-great-curator-great.

## RSS to HTML

This technique is perhaps a bit more technical, but it also allows you the greatest control.

Just about all online content these days comes powered by RSS, making it easy to convert a find into a feed that can be converted into HTML code and displayed on any page.

For example, if you wanted to publish positive mentions of your firm on a new page on your site, you simply set up Google Alerts so that you received notice that your firm was mentioned. Click through to the page, and assuming it's something you want to publish to your site, you would bookmark the content using Pinboard and a tag like "ournews."

Pinboard creates tag-based RSS feeds, so anything you tag with "ournews" can be displayed in a specific RSS feed. This gives you total control over what you want to appear in the feed.

Once you create the feed, you can take it to FeedBurner or RSSinclude to convert the feed to HTML code that you can embed on a page or widget to easily display the content from the feed wherever you choose.

Then anytime you bookmark a new item, it will publish to the page.

## Ask Little Things

One of the best ways to get lots of people to create content for you around a specific topic is to ask lots of people to answer one very short question.

This can be a great way to get lots of suggestions, opinions, and insights collected to support or start a topic of interest to your readers.

The other powerful thing about this approach is that you can often get higher-profile contributors to participate if all you are asking them to do is answer one question or finish one statement.

Once you collect all of your answers, you simply add context and analysis.

It's time to make other people's content one of your teaching-as-selling foundation planks.

# 21

# Building a Platform

**I've reserved this chapter to** discuss what may be one of the biggest ideas in this book.

I believe the future of business and commitment building resides in the idea of viewing your business as a platform for your community. I've spent a great deal of time presenting the idea of going to work on yourself and getting your staff to view the business as their ultimate product. Now I want to leave you with the idea of opening your business as a product for the greater community to embrace and build upon.

I would like to suggest that the notion of a platform is one that we can apply to almost any business and it's certainly a notion that applies to the building of a commitment engine.

## What Is a Platform in This Context?

A platform is a system that helps people create products, services, profits, businesses, communities, and networks of their own. The dynamics that must be present to create a platform environment are openness and collaboration.

So, the questions you need to ponder are:

- How could you or your business act as a platform?
- What could others build on top of your business or products?
- How could you add more value through your platform approach?
- How could you grow a network on your platform?
- Are there other businesses that your platform could launch?
- How could the community generate value for other members of the community?
- How could your platform learn from community members?
- How could you create something open enough to attract your competitors?
- What platforms already exist that you could build on?
- Could you use your existing purpose, culture, or community as a platform?
- What could you acquire as a way to build a platform?
- What could you extend as a way to build a platform?

When you start to think about your business in this manner, you can move beyond the traditional applications of the term *platform* and blend platform-type thinking into your business model, your culture, and ultimately into the way you engage and communicate with your community.

MAYA Design Inc. is a technology design firm and innovation lab founded in Pittsburgh in 1989. MAYA believes in spawning other businesses based on its platform and unique approach. To date, it has started four new companies, an outgrowth of its unique business incubation process that encourages internal research initiatives to spin off as new companies when they become financially independent.

MAYA has been selected as a "Top Small Company to Work for in America" by *Inc.* magazine, *Fortune Small Business,* and *Entrepreneur.*

## Find Your Unique Framework

Appletree Answers has built a platform of sorts by figuring out how
to change the paradigm of the call-center culture. Calls centers
have a long history of employee dissatisfaction and burnout.

Appletree has a decidedly different story when it comes to
employee retention and that's their unique framework for their
industry.

The company's rapid growth has come about by acquiring other
small call centers and installing Appletree's unique framework
based on a strong culture of commitment and beliefs in action.
Appletree's strong culture is what they've built all of their expan-
sion on.

The key is to ground your platform in your unique qualities.
Oftentimes this requires thinking beyond what your core business
was designed to do and looking purely at what you've gotten good
at doing, even if you do these things to support your core business.

For example, Amazon sells lots of books, but in order to do this,
it needed to develop lots of file serving and a huge storage capacity
and get very, very good at delivering lightning-quick Web results in
one of the highest-traffic environments online.

Amazon took something that had little to do with its core business, selling goods online, but which it had become incredibly pro-
ficient at, and created Amazon Web Services, which allows thousands
of businesses to build on the Amazon framework.

One company that is built on Amazon Web Services is Airbnb, a
community marketplace that allows property owners and travelers
to connect with one another for the purpose of renting unique vacation spaces around the world. I use it frequently and love how simple
the service is to use. Airbnb uses these database tools to build their
community.

## It's All About Building More Value

A major dynamic of the platform component is value creation. No matter what your business does, it will sink or swim based on the value (perceived or otherwise) it creates in someone's life. This is extremely important when we talk about the community aspect of a platform.

If you want to differentiate your business from others that are already providing value to a market, you've got to find a way to create more value as a competitive edge. Many people default to adding features to products and services as a way to address this, but I think the real impact in value creation comes from strategically finding ways to add value to a unique experience rather than through some sort of product enhancement.

The beauty of understanding value creation at the strategic level and then forcing that thinking into every tactical decision is that this is some of the most profitable work you can do. When a market comes to value your business as the "go-to" choice, you're on your way to a premium pricing opportunity. People will pay dearly for an experience that helps them get more of what they want out of life.

Below are five ways to think about value creation beyond your core offerings.

**Promote your team.** One of my favorite ways to deliver value is to surround myself with a team of best-of-class providers who can produce every result that my clients need and then play a role in promoting that team to help meet their needs. There's no question that this mind-set makes you more valuable to your clients, but it also makes you more valuable to your team members.

**Goal achievement.** This is something I've always promoted and I think it's actually become easier in the more personal business world we now live in. If you can find logical ways to get your clients to reveal their goals and then go to work on ways to help them reach those goals, even if they are seemingly unrelated to your business, you'll add value that will be hard for competitors to understand.

Few things breed loyalty like a challenge. This approach requires the ability to earn and build trust beyond the traditional business relationship, but if it's done authentically, it can be hard to replicate.

**Teach and loan.** I've always been a big advocate of teaching your customers how to do things they want to know how to do, no matter what it is. If you as a business owner have mastered a skill, even if it's just a better way to get your taxes done, you can add massive value to your client relationships by lending your expertise, skills, and knowledge or by setting up classes to teach other business owners how to do the same. This is also a great way to build a platform for your strategic team members by offering them the opportunity to teach and connect. Become a school and watch your value soar.

**Filter and aggregate.** There is so much out there that is free to use, abuse, and consume that some may wonder how they can actually charge for much of what they offer. The key is the package. Organizations that understand how to deliver information and services in the right amount, order, device, and timing provide so much value that they can actually charge a premium for content by simply putting it in the right place. Every customer, consumer, or business needs better information, no matter what you sell.

**Provide access.** Building a business today means building a community. You can do this through proven techniques like membership offering and training, but you can also do it by giving your customers an opportunity to come together. More often than not, they have the same challenges and backgrounds and may even be in the same industry. Your business could be the perfect platform to facilitate a mutually beneficial network. Some organizations have found that this can become a central element of their offering.

## Build Commitment Through Partnership

This mind-set suggests that a great deal of the organization's platform thinking involves seeking out and activating business partners with the same ideal client target.

Understand that this is much more than simply businesses referring business to one another.

A total partnership model rests on your desire to build a community of providers that you can tap into to provide your clients with access to a best-of-class team. When you look at building a platform for your clients in this manner, your business can become the hub of your clients' world. In addition, with a model that allows others to build on your unique framework, you can build a loyal and committed community of businesses to support your platform.

There are a number of components involved in the creation of an effective partnership.

**Recruit and introduce.** The first step is to recruit your team and introduce them to your program and business. One of the best ways to identify good teammates is to ask your current customers to name other businesses they like to buy from. You don't want just anyone as a partner; these need to be people you can also confidently refer business to.

**Create content opportunities.** Invite your partners to contribute to your newsletter or act as a guest on your podcast or blog. Giving your partners exposure by way of content gets them exposure and you content. Consider taking this up a notch and create a group blog optimized for all of the partners.

**Conduct video interviews.** Set up a meeting with your partners and use the opportunity to record an introduction video so you can have content to run on your Web site letting the world know about your partnership. This will show that you mean business.

**Acquire special offers.** Get your partners to contribute a product or service that you can use as a way to enhance your offering. Free business cards for every logo purchased or free flowers when you make a reservation for dinner, free tickets to give away in your marketing, or a free HVAC checkup when you get some plumbing work. This is a great way to promote your partners while adding real appeal to your own marketing. Make sure you create real value here.

**Make referrals.** Make it a habit to consciously go out of your way to refer business to your partners. Don't wait for people to ask; do it as part of your Monday routine. This is how you become someone who lots of great providers want to partner with, but you also increase your value to your customers by consistently helping them get what they need in every aspect of their life.

**Rate and review.** If at all possible, become a customer of every one of your partners. This will make you a much more authentic referral source (as a user) and allow you to test and promote the truly great experiences. Follow up on this by actively writing reviews and ratings on Yelp and other online sites.

**Create events.** Figure out how to bring your partners together to network and create deeper engagement. Let each partner have a day where they educate everyone in the network. Create workshops and offer to conduct them for your partners' customers. Develop a day devoted to topics that your partners can present useful information on, and have everyone promote the event.

With just a little bit of creativity, any organization can tap the awesome power of a partnership as a substantial lead, customer, and community generator.

# 22

# The Committed Way Revisited

**Now that you've traveled to** this point, let's revisit the steps involved in the creation of your commitment engine.

The following seven elements make up the essence of our exploration in this book. The first three deal with commitment on an intensely personal level; the fourth is the bridge to bringing commitment to your business; and the final three address the practical ways in which you leverage commitment inside your business to create commitment externally through and with your customers.

All seven elements rely on one another to a large degree. You can have one without the others, but you'll never fully realize what's possible without the entire system of elements functioning together.

In fact, as growth occurs, maintaining an established balance among these elements will prove to be one of the greatest challenges. If you've ever worked inside an organization that has experienced rapid growth, you've likely experienced this system falling in and out of balance.

Maybe you don't get to sit around and brainstorm with the founder anymore. Marketing strategy gets confused with marketing tactics. The culture isn't what it used to be when it was just a couple of passionate start-up guys and gals doing whatever needed to be done.

Organizations that go through a hypergrowth period either restore their balance or they continue to expand and contract in painful lurches.

You may recall that in the introduction to this work I mentioned the importance of chaos and the need to embrace it. Balance and chaos will converge and separate at many different points on this journey. The key is to come to view them as signposts of progress and important parts of the system of growth. At least that way they won't make you as crazy.

# 1. Define Your Relationship with the Work

It's hard to do a really good job on anything you don't think about in the shower.

—*Paul Graham, cofounder of Y Combinator*

The first step in the system is to understand your own relationship with the work the business does. In the initial stages, the personality of a business is often completely aligned with that of the owner.

How they view the business, what they want it to be, what they fear, what they desire, how they communicate, how they work with others, and how they view the world in general. Quite often a business, its culture, and the makeup of the clients it attracts are a direct reflection of the owner of the business.

John Ratliff founded Appletree Answers, a telephone-answering service and call center, in 1995 in the spare room of a two-bedroom apartment.

It was a business he knew little about but had developed an interest in as a result of a relationship with an equipment vendor. He sold his existing cellular-phone business and entered an entirely new industry with little more than desire.

By his own admission, he fumbled along and teetered on the brink of going under. His business provided telephone-answering services and his clients needed their phones answered day and night. He did everything in the business including working the phones.

He had patched together a handful of on-again, off-again staff members but worked many of the evening shifts himself. He tells of many nights when he grabbed a little sleep between calls and suffered from near exhaustion most days.

One early morning at around four o'clock, the phone rang and he felt as though he couldn't take it anymore. He woke up, walked to the closet that housed his phone system, and began to yank the power cord from the wall.

All of a sudden he felt as though he had been struck by an abnormal sense of calm and an irrational confidence that told him all he needed to do was answer this call and everything was going to be fine. He actually talks now about seeing a vision of a future, in that moment, in which everything worked out.

He answered the call with newfound certainty only to learn that the caller had dialed the wrong number.

He laughs now as he tells this story and claims that most of the time people find it a bit hard to believe, but that was the day he reignited his passion and renewed his commitment to build what is now one of the most successful call-center operations in North America.

In order for a business to become fully alive, the owner of the business must be fully alive. He must have passion and desire for his work, but he must also be able to connect what he does on a daily basis with his own personal needs.

He must be able to connect his vision for his business with his vision for his life, if only faintly at first.

A business owner must be able to see his business as a place that can help him develop his capacity for things like purpose, love, wonder, courage, and grace.

I frequently ask business owners to list the one thing they love most about owning a business and the majority boil it down to one word: *freedom*. While freedom can take many forms and include many things, I believe the freedom to grow who you are as a human being is perhaps the most tangible form of freedom that exists.

## 2. Discover Your Higher Purpose Served by the Work

Mitch Joel, partner and president of Toronto-based digital marketing agency Twist Image, followed a rather unusual path to his current business.

Joel told me what he calls his "jagged journey" like this:

> I knew from a very early age that I had a passion to build something and that I needed to be a millionaire before I turned twenty. I had a real passion for music, so I started writing for music magazines and one day decided to start my own. I had no idea what I was doing, so I just started calling around to various publication editors and for some reason one took pity on me and explained how everything worked. In 1992, I put the magazine on the Internet and thought I was about to change the world of publishing. The magazine never really took off, but I learned how important the online world would become, so I took a job selling online ads, founded a record label, and started helping brands with online promotion. All of my random passions came together to lead me to help launch Twist Image. I believe the work that I do right now is the art I was meant to express.

Like Joel, once you establish the reasons for starting a business and the ways that business might enrich your life, it's time to focus on how you will develop your own personal commitment inside that business and how it serves your higher purpose.

For the most part, business can be pretty boring. You go to work, you make stuff, you ship stuff, you get paid, and everyone is happy, right?

The thing that makes a business exciting is purpose. While it's great to love what you do, if you're ever going to generate commitment from others, and if your business is to become fully alive, you've got to understand why you do what you do. You must find the higher purpose that your work has to offer and translate that into something that can move others to join your cause.

While there is plenty of room to define what a term like *higher purpose* might mean to someone individually, there's little doubt that organizations that enjoy the highest level of commitment are able to communicate a reason for being that contributes to the greater good.

That reason for being may or may not relate directly to the goods or services the company produces, but it always stands as the single reason for why people connect at a deeper level.

This idea is an evolving one in most organizations and usually starts with the spark of an idea or is born out of a significant event. Over time and through experiences both good and bad, and as a result of bouts of internal examination, purpose often reveals itself to those who watch for it.

In this element of the system, we will go to work on discovering purpose and developing habits to keep it real, ever present, and continuously evolving.

## 3. Install Purpose as a Meaningful Way for Others to Connect with Your Business

Once you're able to find your own higher purpose, the real reason the business exists, and the element that connects your business to your life, you've got to install that purpose in your business in a way that is meaningful to others.

It's not always easy and there are plenty of people who will suggest you shouldn't even try. This is where it gets tricky. The thing that drives you can be very personal, it can be very hard to explain, and it may not even feel very businesslike, but that's the point.

The creative work required to connect your intentions with a community, message, brand, and culture is what makes the difference in the degree to which people are attracted, connected, and committed to your business.

This is where we will begin the work of turning your business into a community—one built on purpose. The best communities are those that form around ideas and causes. In this case, the single-minded purpose for why your business exists is this profound idea and cause you must develop.

The group that ultimately forms around this idea may include a large and varied set of relationships with employees, networks, circles, friends, followers, prospects, customers, suppliers, advisers, and even competitors, something James Moore equated to a business ecosystem in *The Death of Competition:* "Over time, they coevolve their capabilities and roles, and tend to align themselves with the directions set by one or more central companies."*

## 4. Lead by Telling Stories

The next element in the system is the bridge element. This is where you will take your own personal passion and commitment that were generated and defined in the first three elements of the system, and use them to get others to join your cause.

The best leaders are simply some of the best storytellers. High-profile examples such as Steve Jobs, Herb Kelleher, and Richard Branson abound, but the ability to use stories as a way to generate purpose and commitment is available to anyone.

Building a bridge from your own personal commitment to generating commitment in your staff and your customers depends on your ability and willingness to lead by crafting and telling stories to your community.

---

* James Moore, *The Death of Competition: Leadership and Strategy in the Age of Business Ecosystems* (New York: HarperBusiness, 1997).

Full commitment comes about when you involve your staff and customers in the process of storytelling and story building.

## 5. Build Your Business Around the Characteristics of Real-Life Strategy

The final steps in the system address the tangible ways you manifest, foster, and balance commitment in your fully alive business through strategy, culture, and customer.

While the idea of strategy is bantered about liberally in business, I rarely find a business owner who can apply strategy in the abstract way it's generally presented. Let me ask you this: what is strategy exactly?

People commit to things that are simple, inspirational, convenient, innovative, playful, community-oriented, and filled with surprise. These are the characteristics of a real-life business and marketing strategy, and these are the characteristics that a fully alive business must use as its everyday language.

Find a way to wrap your purpose in these characteristics and build a community that's drawn to that purpose and you will be on the surest path to creating a commitment-filled business.

This is what marketers commonly refer to as positioning, and while it's often thought of in terms of product features and competitive strategies, it is most effective when delivered and experienced using traits that resemble a business's personality rather than the effective allocation of resources.

Embrace these seven characteristics—simplicity, inspiration, convenience, innovation, play, community, and surprise—as your collaborators in all you do. They can act as your touchstones for every business strategy and decision in the most practical ways possible.

# 6. Make Culture Your Greatest Marketing Asset

Never doubt that a small group of thoughtful, committed people can change the world. Indeed, it is the only thing that ever has.

—*Margaret Mead, author of* Culture and Commitment

As any business grows, the customer experience often moves away from the passion and commitment of the owner into the hands of staff members.

As this occurs, if you are unable to breed a level of commitment in your staff, you will find it next to impossible to create any level of commitment in your customers.

In this element of the system, we move into exploring the work required to create an internal business environment where a commitment culture flourishes.

So many businesses fail by assuming that culture must be created through handbooks, signs, and speeches. A culture of commitment grows when employees are viewed as the first community members and the first customers of the business.

Your staff needs to feel your commitment as much as you do. They need to appreciate the story you connect to your higher purpose for the business. Some employees may be attracted simply by the way you exhibit your own commitment, but all must be given the opportunity to connect to the single-minded purpose of the business. Use the seven characteristics above to draw out the connection and to develop strategy.

Company policy, meetings, hiring, and management should have a guiding set of principles, but if it's not simple, inspiring, convenient, innovative, fun, community-based, and surprise-filled, it doesn't make the cut.

When this is done systematically, strategy informs culture and culture becomes strategy.

## 7. Orchestrate Commitment in Every Element of the Brand

The final element of the system involves the public face of a business: the marketing experienced by customers and prospects.

It should come as no surprise that we encounter the seven characteristics of commitment here again, as they hold the key to fulfilling the promise that runs through strategy, culture, and customer.

We use these characteristics to make customer service decisions, product decisions, promotion decisions, design decisions, and even price decisions. The game remains the same.

In a fully alive, commitment-filled business, the customer is, in effect, a manifestation of everything the characteristics of commitment have to offer. The business becomes fully alive when a customer experiences it through the intentional acts of simplicity, inspiration, convenience, innovation, play, community, and surprise.

Let's start building your committed business.

# Conclusion

**There can be no life,** passion, or purpose in a business that lacks commitment. I've proposed in this text that I believe commitment or failure to commit is one of the central themes of our lives.

It is what drives us forward and drives us away. It is what provides us with passion and fuels our greatest fears. It is what guides us to take a road less traveled or herds us onto the deeply rutted path.

Commitment isn't about projects or events; it's a long-term game. In fact, it may really be a lifelong game. But it's not about being committed to one thing no matter what. It's not even about staying committed to only one thing.

It's about searching for the deeper meaning of your life and bringing what you find to every moment that you can, to your business, to your employees, and to your community.

I am committed to my business, but when I say this, I'm not saying that I'm committed to growing it to a specific size or stature. Instead, I'm committed to the idea that I can help small-business owners find their purpose and passion through my words and my work even when I'm not sure what my next move should be.

Commitment isn't about the daily grind; it's about clarity, control, and consent.

In order to possess the kind of commitment that will serve you, serve those around you, and ultimately serve your business, you must be crystal clear about what you believe and why and you must put those beliefs into action in every decision. You must develop a sense of control about where you are headed but release a great deal of control about how you'll arrive there. You must give yourself permission to learn and grow and evolve with the help of others.

Until your sense of commitment is infused with these three things there will always be uncertainty.

Above all else, there can be no real commitment until you surrender all doubt.

# Acknowledgments

My family for encouragement dosed with a share of humility

My girls for laughing with me and at me

My customers for teaching me about mutual respect

My readers for having the courage to express their opinions

Steve for sharing my work with the publishing world

Coffee Girls for one too many breakfast burritos

The Kansas City, Missouri, Public Library for remaining so utterly relevant

Emily for shortening my sentences in a very good way

David for suggesting I write this book

Hugh for daily inspiration and an office full of art

Seth for your example of generosity

Stephen for telling me what fear is here to say

Hoss for never judging me or anyone else

# Index